Business Before Craft

BUSINESS BEFORE CRAFT

How to let go of the art and become a working actor

SARA MORNELL

Copyright © 2020 Sara Mornell

All rights reserved.

This document is geared towards providing exact and reliable information in regards to the topic and issue covered.

No part of this book may be reproduced in any form or by any electronic or mechanical means including information storage and retrieval systems, without permission in writing from the author. The only exception is by a reviewer, who may quote short excerpts in a review.

The trademarks that are used are without any consent, and the pub- lication of the trademark is without permission or backing by the trade- mark owner. All trademarks and brands within this book are for clarifying purposes only and are owned by the owners themselves, not affiliated with this document.

DEDICATION

To all the actors who put their trust in The Mornell Method and believe in the work I am doing. This book is a reminder that I am always in your corner.

With Love,
Coach Mornell

CONTENTS

Dedication 5
Forward 9
Chapter 1: **Setting The Foundation** 15
Chapter 2: **If The Door's Closed, Use The Window** 21
Chapter 3: **Perfecting Your Package** 25
Chapter 4: **Speak Agent** 33
Chapter 5: **Class** 43
Chapter 6: **Before The Audition** 49
Chapter 7: **Addressing The Room** 55
Chapter 8: **Self Tapes** 69
Chapter 9: **Atlanta** 75
Conclusion 79
Interviews 83
    Jennifer Cooper 84
    Ethan Embry 96
    Jason Lockhart 103
    Jesse Williams 112
    Christina Ochoa 117
    Sherry Thomas 124
About The Author 133

"Sara is passionate about the business of this industry. She's tough because she cares - she's effective because she's smart - people trust her because she's sincere. I have seen first hand the results of her coaching, and I trust her methods completely. As an agent, one question that I get consistently is "Who should I train with?" My answer is just as consistent - "Sara Mornell" With common sense, tough love and incredible instincts, Sara has taught my clients how to intelligently navigate this industry, and to be confident in their choices."

Jessica Talley
Talent Agent

FORWARD

Dear Actors,

If you have ever sat in yet another acting class wondering, "how is this going to help me book work?" you are not alone. If you have taken years of class, but cannot successfully apply what you've learned to a real world audition, you are not alone. You are among hundreds of thousands of frustrated actors.

If the business side of it all scares you, but you are tired of being a professional class taker then I wrote this for you. And for the thousands who are looking for a way to break into the business but are getting nowhere, I wrote this book for you too. The endless cycle of taking classes built on antiquated theater techniques is big business, and one that does not **help** actors. That infuriated me, and at the same time was breaking my heart so I set out on working for change. Actors must understand and come to terms with the business of the entertainment industry or the chance of succeeding diminishes rapidly.

In Sally Fields' book, In Pieces she talks about studying with Lee Strasbourg but after a decade of training realizing that, that work did not help her understand the art of the audition. Her coach David Craig in **1975** said, "most directors or whoever is sitting in the casting chair, rarely look(ed) for the best actor to play the part, but instead waited for the actual character to walk through the door. Only when an actor with enough recognition is attached, will they be given the opportunity to play a character unlike the very person that they appear to be. And even then, it's rare." That was in 1975. So why then does the training continue to focus on teaching actors how to act like other people? Because 90% of the training out there is based and insists on teaching theater techniques to actors working in an entirely different medium.

That is why I created the Mornell Method, to revolutionize the way actors train. Training that is based on teaching people how to find all the versions of their authentic selves. Life teaches us to act, audition rooms teach us to act, and classes teach us to act... I teach people how to be fearless in who they are. There is no shame AT ALL in only wanting to do film and TV. I am a classically trained actor, and that used to mean something. To some extent it still does. However, what I have found is that more often than not, I am working to undo years of training and get my actors to stop acting. That being said, this book is not about the actual Mornell Method - this is a book to break down what you need to do in order to get represented and how to be the type of actor agents want to represent. In short, hopefully it helps you get your sh*t together.

Seriously - if you only get one thing from the book let it be this. STOP BEING DESPERATE. There is no quick fix or overnight success here. When you are desperate to be signed or to book, that energy is not only completely obvious, it literally keeps you from booking and representation.

I encourage you to stand for more than just a selfie, and not to limit yourself to just being an actor. That day and age has come and gone. As creatives we are capable of doing so much more, of wearing many different hats. Embrace that. It may take 10-20 years of auditioning before you are able to support yourself through your acting alone- and even that is a *near impossible* achievement. Near impossible, not impossible. I see miracles happen every week as a coach - to be a part of changing someone's life is a gift. I hope this book gives you some of the answers that you have been seeking and I look forward to working with you..

PREFACE

As an actor you are the CEO of your own company. The day and age of the art/craft of acting on film being the most important part of training stopped being a reality decades ago. Viewing Hollywood from this lens is a vital shift for your success. The business has changed drastically in the past decade, and will only continue to do so. My goal is to give actors a no bullshit straight talking guide to educate them about the reality of "show business." I think people are seeking answers that work for today's working actors. It is heartbreaking to meet an actor who has been in the industry for years but still has not learned the business and how it works. My feeling is that if we accurately educate actors then we will see stronger more confident artists and that is instrumental for launching a successful career. This book is about breaking myths and misconceptions about the entertainment industry and helping you dominate the 2% of what is within your control. I want to stop the endless cycle of actors getting taken advantage of. You can be the best actor in the world, but when you don't know the business that is Hollywood, you will only go so far. I train my actors like athletes-and have found that to be a key to success. When we meld the creative spirit with the athletic frame of mind we can win the game that is Hollywood.

CHAPTER 1

Setting The Foundation

Once you've made the decision, get into the Olympic frame of mind. It's a trail of blood, sweat, and tears — no different than any athlete.

TUNNEL YOUR VISION

People think acting is easy. It's not. With any big life decision, there are assessments to make first. Before entering medical school, you would need to be pretty sure that you wanted to be a doctor. The same goes for acting. Be prepared that it can take a minimum of ten years before you achieve any kind of success. It takes twenty to become an "overnight success". In those years you will experience rejections, moments of doubt, financial burden and stress. It's a hard life. It's a hard path, which is not necessarily a bad thing. When actors are comfortable, they stop growing.

Is it hard to work an eight-hour shift at a restaurant and get up in the morning for an audition? Is it hard to say no to your best friend's birthday party because a last-minute audition comes up? Is it hard to be on your way to the airport and get an email that you have a callback and make a decision to turn around and cancel your trip? Will you need to get up, with very little sleep, in order to coach? Will you need to miss family vacations to be available? Will this be one of the hardest things you've ever done in your life? Does hearing the three words "you booked it" make it all worth it? YES.

When I was 13, I was told by a very famous actress, "If I can talk you out of being an actor today, tomorrow, or over the next three days, then you will not be an actor. You have to have it in your heart, your soul, your blood, and your veins. If that's you, then enjoy your career. If you are wavering in your decision to be an actor even slightly, then you will be much happier pursuing a different path." What you will need to do is to tunnel your vision.

When you're worried about bills, transportation, not looking your best, or drama with a friend, it's a distraction and fucks with your focus. Anything outside of your career that is a distraction will keep you from achieving your goals. A boyfriend, girlfriend, roommate situation, money job that takes all your time and attention, or backup plan, all can hurt you or keep you from what it is that you actually want to do. Like anything in life, if you let what you can control interfere with your pursuit, then it will do just that. And if that's the case, if that's your situation, I would say you don't really want to be an actor.

I tell my actors to train like they are preparing for the Olympics. Lose the excuses, focus on training, and discipline yourselves. Be prepared to work harder at this than anything else in the world. If you're not prepared to bust your ass then find a different profession. It might cold and harsh, but that's the truth and that's what it takes. Welcome to Hollywood.

And now that I have just pissed all over your hopes and dreams, let's get started.

CREATE A HOME BASE

This industry is going to beat you to shit. The sooner you accept that, the easier your path will be. A business based in rejection requires that you have a steady, serene environment that is your castle, that is your fortress.

Your home, whether that's a garage, a studio, or a five-bedroom house, has to provide you a sanctuary.

There is so much about this industry that is unstable, we never know where were going to be day to day or what we're going to be called upon to do. If you're reading this now, and you don't have a solid situation set up for yourself in terms of where you live, put that at the top of your priority list. This also includes the people in your home or for that matter, in your life. I tell actors all the time that if you have someone in your life that's not supporting this, get rid of them. That might sound harsh, but what I want for you to realize is that actors are gladiators going into the ring to fight for their lives. This is a competition.

For every role, there are thousands of people submitting. You need to be able to work without distraction. If your home environment is the distraction, then not only is it not beneficial, it is damaging. If you have drama or negativity coming from your surroundings or the people in your life, now is the time to remedy it.

We as actors tend to be impulsive and reactive. My advice is to slow down and do your due diligence. Ask to crash on peoples couches if needed, but don't jump into a roommate situation off of Craigslist, only to have someone to turn out to be psycho or crazy six months later. That being said, try not to spend all of your paycheck on rent.

Early on in my career, a seasoned actor offered me some solid advice. He said, "Do not waste your money on rent." I had just booked a show and chose not to take his advice. When the pilot got picked up, I rented a house in Beverly Hills that cost $3600 a month. Cut to me getting a call from my agent saying the network had just put out a breakdown to recast my role. They wanted someone whiter and thinner. I had suddenly gone from, "You're going to be making $40,000 an episode," to, "You don't have a job."

We as humans need a safe space, and for actors, it should be a job requirement. If this is absolutely not available to you in this moment, then work to find a space that gives you quiet, serenity, and peace. A place that allows you to focus and recover. Get serious about your space, just do it without selling your soul.

GET A MONEY JOB

Every cent you earn must be reinvested back into you, whether that's for a great photographer, dentist, gas, personal trainer, Pilates, dermatologist, acting coach, or dialect coach. This is a career based on looks and the camera picks up on everything. You cannot wait until you are working and successful to look and feel your best. Just as a business owner would invest in his product, you must invest in yourself, and that takes money.

You'll need a job that gives you enough flexibility to go to auditions and get your self-tapes submitted efficiently and without stress. Most people work in a restaurant because you work a night shift. A money job, whether it's bartending, modeling, tutoring, babysitting, or working as a security guard, simply needs to give you an income. That being said, stop complaining about your money job. Of course you'd rather be working on set, but you aren't there yet, so look at what you have and make the most of it. Rather than complaining, use it as fuel to help you accomplish your dream. Make it your time to act. The more interesting, charismatic, funny, charming, or 'on' you are with people, the farther you'll go and the more they'll tip you.

If your waiting tables, read your audience. If it's a table full of older women, instead of saying you're an actor, slip in that you're going to school to get a nursing degree. Maybe you want to go into pediatrics or hospice care. Change your profession, change your story, play with your tables / audience / boss. Try it for a week. Shift what you say to account for who you're talking to. Instead of being reactive and defensive, be proactive and figure out the audience and create a story. Actors, at their core, need to be storytellers. Use this time to see how many versions of yourself you can authentically connect to. If your money job is making you miserable, sick, or stressed, then it's time for you to take a risk and make a change. Actors limit themselves, and yet, being a creative person means that we are capable of much more than just acting. What else are you passionate about? What else are you good at? What else do you love? (And if you're saying "Nothing! Only acting!", then you are in for a very long and hard journey. Stop limiting yourself and find something else.). An actress I worked with started her own candle company from the bottles that were thrown out from the clubs she used to work in. She went from bottle service to a being successful small business owner. And by the way, www.afterthepartycandleco.com is her site. Check it out.

Get out of feeling miserable and ask yourself, "Where else can I be creative in my life and how can I get paid for it?". If you are in fear financially, it can be absolutely crippling. This leads to desperation; if you walk into rooms or do your self-tapes while worrying about money, then you are coming from a place of fear, doubt and insecurity. I want you to look for ways you can be creatively satisfied and happy outside of booking jobs through the industry. That being said, you cannot be lazy. You have to be prepared to work harder at this than anybody else. Work ethic is highly underdeveloped in most actors. If you have found yours, then you are already ahead of the game.

CHAPTER 2

If The Door's Closed, Use The Window

The most important thing you won't hear in an acting class:
Get representation, Now.

If I haven't been clear already, let me state the obvious: I go against what actors have conventionally been told and been taught. The system is broken and what I teach is how to not fall into the traps of antiquated bullshit.

I don't understand the point of keeping actors in class if they aren't actively auditioning. If an actor doesn't have representation, then they should not be in class.

Actors shy away from seeking out representation, sometimes because they don't know how, but more often than not, it comes from a fear of being rejected. If your class isn't pushing you past your comfort zone and sense of security, then it is time to find another class. Actors are paying anywhere from $200-600 dollars a month, learning scene study, Meisner, and stage combat, but have no idea how to audition. The only way to book is through auditioning. The way to get that audition is through representation. Now, if you're reading this and do not have representation, my hope would be that you are submitting yourself. If you aren't auditioning enough, start submitting yourself. The first piece of film on my demo-reel came from a USC graduate short film I submitted myself for. Until you have an agent who is busting their ass for you, you have to be busting your own.

First and foremost, do not submit yourself too early. You have to have perfect package. Once you decide it's the right time for you to submit to an agency, look to see how they prefer for actors to submit. Pay attention to the details and follow their instructions to the letter. It important for us as a community to step it up. The old school actor was artistic and kind of a mess. The actor I train, the new kind of actor, is compulsive, type-A, and has an athletic frame of mind. It's what my actors would call being a Mornellian. It amazes me that in a business where professionalism is everything, most actors have none. Actors have given themselves a bad rap Stop doing that. Pay attention to the small details. It goes a long way in this industry. So how do you get representation?

Option One

Once your materials are phenomenal – two to three great headshots that show who you are and the type you play, one to three minutes of footage on tape (this can be a self-tape), and a currently updated and perfect Actors Access and IMDB – ask someone who is with an agent you want to refer you. Be aware and smart about what agents you target. Unless you are 18, gorgeous, and have a famous family, CAA is not going to sign you. When you are starting out, target boutique agencies.

Option Two

Look for agents or casting directors who graduated from your high school or college. Alma mater matters. Ask to take them to lunch or coffee and see if you can get their advice. Do not go into that meeting asking for them to submit you. Ask for opinion. If they offer to look at your materials, have them at the ready. Assuming of course, that your materials are updated, phenomenal, and ready to go.

Option Three

Similar to option one, ask your friends and classmates for recommendations. Some actors will get really squirrelly about this, so maybe don't ask your doppelganger. If they say yes, make it easy for them to forward your materials in a simple and professional email.

Option Four

Theatre. I've seen actors get signed by Gersh after seeing actors in a musical or show. As long as it's a top-notch production, theatre is still a great way to get seen.

Option Five

Do your research. Find the top ten or twenty agencies in the market you live in. Go to IMDB and see the people on their roster and look for people who look like you. If they don't have any or only have a few, submit to them. Don't do a cover letter, it's pointless. Clearly, you are looking for representation, why else would you be sending your picture and resume? What you can do is include a nice card if it is sent via the mail. Keep it short, one to three sentences, being cognizant that agents have very little time on their hands.

Option Six

If you're in class, make sure your coach has industry connections. Talk to you teachers about who they can refer you to.

Option Seven

Work with a career coach. Like with anything, please do your research and ensure that they have clients that you admire and have a proven track record.

The Rare Option That Does Happen

Get discovered. I've had people be discovered on the street, behind a bar, bagging groceries, and everywhere in between. I once had a student who was 35, had no credits, and was discovered on Hollywood Boulevard. His presence on the street was so charismatic that it convinced a manager to hand over a card and say, "call me". When you go out into the world, don't hide behind a baseball hat and sweats. Agents always tell me they're looking for the next big thing.

CHAPTER 3

Perfecting Your Package

Know you are a product. Stop being so artsy fartsy. Hollywood will Give you a label. Don't fight it.

Your first step toward getting representation is to create an outstanding package to present. What exactly does that mean? First, determine your type. Then have a phenomenally accurate picture, write a unique resumé, and have a reel that people besides your mom would actually want to watch.

Something is going on with all actors, and I'm not exactly sure why, nor can I pinpoint the reason it has reached epidemic proportions (which it has), and that something is called desperation. Last week, my agent shared with me a small fraction of the emails that he receives every day from actors wanting to be represented by his agency. To be blunt, the emails are delusional. These are emails, strewn with errors, reading "hi, I'm so and so and im a really talented actor can you rep me? Attached is a photo". And he gets hundreds if not thousands of this type of email every month. That is absolutely, in my mind, inexcusable. Yet it happens frighteningly often (our office gets similar emails as well, even though we aren't an agency). So, let me be very clear: there is no magic pill. There is no quick fix. This isn't a career of overnight success.

We as a community need to demand professionalism from ourselves and those we surround ourselves with. In no other industry would someone apply for a job in the same way that actors seek representation. In the real world, if someone applied for a job (whether that be waiting tables or working for a law firm) in this manner, there would be no preliminary interview and most likely their application would be tossed. Now, this is exactly what agents do when they receive that type of submission as well. Professionalism is the minimum requirement.

Next, you have to know who you are and how you fit into the Hollywood stereotypes, and which versions of yourself is most marketable. As far as I'm concerned, that is more important for someone entering into film and TV than taking a two-year Meisner class. Recently while doing a Q&A, an actress raised her hand and asked how she could get representation. What I suggested, and what I do suggest, is once you understand your types, or in Mornellian language – the versions of yourself that you can believably play – look up agents and or managers in your area and go through their roster on IMDB. See if they rep anyone who is a similar type to you, and if they have only a few or no one like you, keep them in consideration. I suggested she seek boutique agencies and stay away from the top four. I would recommend that any new actors consider smaller boutique agencies that are interested in developing talent. Afterwards, this actress came up to me and expressed concern. She said, "What if I've already done that, and I don't look different than anyone else. What if I'm the same type or don't know my type." This goes back to the idea of being professional, considerate, and not being desperate. So many agents, casting directors, and managers have told me how hard it is to be corned by actors everywhere they go, and it needs to stop. Getting back to my original point, which is learning where you fit in Hollywood: if you aren't sure what your type is, either hire a career coach or start watching more TV and figure it out for yourself. The whole first three months of LEARN at my studio is spent teaching actors how to discover that for themselves. In general, I think that's something that actors need to focus more on, in a realistic, pragmatic way. That being said, lets figure out how to create an outstanding package.

KNOW WHAT YOU'RE SELLING

Start watching TV. Start with the networks: ABC, NBC, CBS, FOX. Where do you fit? Where do you see actors who look similar to you? What kinds of roles are they booking? Be realistic. If you look more like you belong in the marching band, not as the homecoming queen, then take note of that and start looking for variations of that role / type in other shows. I encourage my students to write four breakdowns. This is not how you see yourself, but how the industry will. Be specific. Create a list of five shows. This is the bare minimum. Would I encourage you to do this for every show you watch? Absolutely. Write a breakdown for yourself for each show. Start with a co-star. Then recurring co-star. Move on to guest star. Recurring guest star. Series regular. Once again, be specific.

For example, a recurring co-star on Modern Family could have you cast Gloria's distant cousin from Columbia who wears glasses with frizzy hair; a quiet wallflower who gets a makeover by Gloria or becomes her clone. Look at any of the Chicago PD, Chicago Fire, Chicago Whatever-The- Fuck shows (formulaic episodic) and see where you would fit in as a guest star. These shows aren't breaking the mold, and as made obvious by the name, all follow a distinct formula. Figuring out where you fit in the equation is not an impossible task, it just takes time and common sense.

Now, if you're already an auditioning actor, I highly recommend doing this exercise no matter what, but I also strongly suggest looking at your past year of breakdowns. You can probably boil them all down to three to five "characters" that you consistently go in for. The breakdowns are what we use when prepping for a headshot session. The more work you do here, the more specific you are about the types of roles you embody, the better your session will go and the happier your representation will be about the specificity of the shots.

A PHENOMENALLY ACCURATE PICTURE

I see actors who take shortcuts. The worst mistake an actor can make is doing this with their headshots. Please don't let a friend with a camera shoot you. You get what you pay for, and a great headshot is the most important tool that you have to get in the door. This is an investment – one of the essentials. Once a year, until you're known as an actor, you need to be getting and updating your headshots. Do not expect that the photographer will tell you your type. Don't expect anyone to tell you your type (including an acting coach at a free Q&A).

If you desperately need help in branding and marketing, then invest in a career coach before getting new headshots. In terms of a photographer: research, research, research. Invest time and energy into finding the right photographer for you. You could tell this by looking at their portfolio. Someone who shot great pics of your best friend may not necessarily be the right fit for you. Take your time and really comb through your options, and when at all possible, meet your photographer before the actual shoot. One of my agents has great advice when it comes to capturing yourself in a headshot.

He says, "it should look like the best candid that you've ever taken while out on the town, or even an amazing selfie you've taken at home." Your headshot absolutely has to look like you. While that seems obvious, countless actors will walk through my door and I don't recognize them because they look so different from their headshot. If you have cystic acne, see a dermatologist and have it taken care of, not airbrushed out so that when you walk into a room the casting director knows they are unable to hire you and subsequently puts you on a list of people not to call again, all because your headshot looks so different from what you actually look like. If you're on a photographer's website and notice that all of the actors look perfect with zero flaws, lots of makeup and heavy lighting, I would caution you away from that style and towards someone who captures an actor's natural look and essence.

PREPARE FOR THE SHOOT

Look your best. Don't drink alcohol or soda. Exercise. Cleanse. See a dermatologist. Make sure your teeth are white. No salt. Think of yourself as an athlete prepping for competition. My suggestion would be to take three outfits for each of the breakdowns that you've chosen for yourself. Give your photographer options, and don't wait until the night before to decide on clothing. If you don't have enough wardrobe options, go to the store and buy clothes. Shoot with the tags still on.

A brief side note – as stated before, boil down the roles you go in for as three to five characters / professions. Then an effective time saver (and the only way to deduct outfits from taxes) is to have three to five outfits that you only use for auditions and are your 'go to' outfits. Its draining to constantly race to find something to wear every time you audition. Your clothes shouldn't distract from your expression or thought. Stay away from anything too busy like polka dots or patterns.

THINKING THE THOUGHT

A head shot is not a modeling picture. A picture can be absolutely stunning but completely wrong. Without the right thought, it's just a pretty picture.

Mike Fenton C.S.A. (*Total Recall, Aliens. Blade Runner, Indiana Jones Trilogy*) an old school casting director gave me some invaluable advice when I was just starting out; he told me that when goes through submissions, what most makes an actor stand out is not how they look, but what they're thinking. It's something actors tend to bypass, yet can be the difference between a good versus phenomenal shoot. What you want to do is look at your breakdowns and have a few ideas about what this person could be thinking. More specifically, a motto or mantra. Mirror the character. If a breakdown calls for a "tough, no nonsense female cop in an all-male task force", my thought might be as simple as "fuck off" or "you're going down". The trick to having a great thought is keeping it to under five words. In the past, actors have focused on having a serious or theatrical shot as opposed to a smiling or commercial shot. But, as mentioned before, it has more to do with what is behind your eyes than what your face is doing. One of my personal tricks is to place my chin wherever the photographer needs it to be so that the actual shot looks good, and then I look down only with my eyes and give myself a beat to have the thought. For a mid-western single mom, whose husband is at war, that thought might be "I miss you". I'll give myself the beat, have the thought, and when I look up that thought is present and allows the photographer to capture that moment.

I also find music incredibly helpful when creating particular versions of myself. Taking the time to make a playlist for my shoot is just taking yourself to the next level of the competition. You cannot over prepare for headshots.

Bottom Line: Anytime someone looks at your picture, they should know exactly how to cast you.

A UNIQUE RESUMÉ

If you don't have an impressive resumé, then start auditioning for student films, web series, spec commercials, indie films, and anything else you can do. Agents do look at what training you've had. Workshops should not go under training, yet I see more and more actors putting the workshops they've attended under this category. This is not something considered training by most people in the industry, and it makes you look green. If you have been a workshop actor and have a relationship with the casting directors, that's something you can mention once you get a meeting. Commercials don't belong on your resumé. Extra work is not something that should be mentioned on a resumé if you are looking to book serious roles. I have never put my height, weight, or eye color on my resumé. That's for modeling. Some agents do require this, but it is up to you whether you want it on your resumé. Let's say you don't have any credits for your resumé. Now it is time to get creative. That doesn't mean lie, it means bump up your *special skills* portion. For example:

Special Skills: pro marksman, horseback rider, stage combat training, zombie training, amateur makeup artist, creative baker, excellent kisser, kid whisperer, therapist-like listening skills, animal faces, Irish, Eastern European, French, Southern, and New York dialects, ability to act possessed by a demon and speak a little Latin on command, gardening, intermediate yoga, singing, hiking, sewing, animal advocate, dog lover, camping, snorkeling (nearly able to scuba dive), strong bullshit detector, chameleon-like dating skills, voice match for porn star Jenna Jameson, pro World peace

If I was an agent and an actor sent me an awesome picture, and I flipped it over to see one credit and eighty special skills, most likely I would laugh and read it. If I liked your look, I would schedule a meeting.

I feel like this is stating the obvious, but make sure the formatting is good. Make sure everything is lined up, it's no more than one page, there are no spelling or grammatical errors, and it generally looks like the resumé of an actor who has their shit together, not someone just starting out who is desperate to be signed. Being type A and compulsive goes a lot farther in this industry than actors realize.

A REEL PEOPLE WOULD WATCH. NOT JUST YOUR MOM

A reel does not have to be something that has aired on TV or is out in theatres. I've had agents use self-tapes that I've done to pitch actors, and that is starting to happen more often. If you haven't worked professionally, go through your self-tapes and see if you have something that accurately represents your work. It must be well lit, have perfect sound, and outstanding quality to be used as a reel. A reel should be under three minutes, three to five minutes max. If you don't have footage from your work or a self-tape, it is time to film some. Find something that is age appropriate and stay away from filming a well-known seen. Nobody wants to see your take on The Notebook, and don't do anything that has won an Academy Award or is generally popular. You're not going to do it better than who they already cast or won the academy award for their performance.

There are companies that do actor demo reels; that's fine and it works, but be careful and diligent about who you hire. Like finding a photographer, you need to do your research. If the quality doesn't match something you would see in film, TV, or an amazing self-tape, then it isn't worth the investment. In LA and New York, check your local colleges or graduate schools for student films or graduate thesis projects. These are always worthwhile in terms of experience or getting great footage. People ask me when to stop taking on free work. My advice is do projects that you love and work with people you like as often as you can. One of the first projects I worked on was a short film from a graduate student at USC. This ended up being invaluable footage for me and it stayed on my reel even after I had several network television and film credits. Work begets work whether you're getting paid or not.

Chapter 4

Speak Agent

Remember when you were a teenager and you got busted for coming home at 2:00 a.m.? Or maybe that sort of sick feeling you got in your stomach when you cheated on a test? Meeting with an agent is kind of like that.

You need an agent. Obviously, you need an agent. This is where most actors trip and fall. And they fall hard. It is one of the most important aspects of our career, and yet actors often procrastinate or stay with a lazy or ineffective agent for much too long. Getting an agent means that you have to actually sell yourself. Which is another thing that actors are notoriously terrible at. So, if you aren't sure about your type or where you fit in the industry or the kinds of roles you would audition for and what stereotypes you'll play, then my suggestion would to be to look for a business consultant or career coach first. We stopped calling this a craft decades ago, and in order to have an amazing agent, you have to understand the business and how best to market yourself. That being said, if you have a phenomenal package, then you are ready to start looking for representation. Let's get started.

Back in the dark ages, when I started, agents were looking for new talent to develop. Part of an agent's job description was guiding an actor's career.

Agents are now looking for a distinct person or a personality, not an actor transforming into a character. This is why we have fewer classically trained actors who are working than we have people who are Instagram influencers or reality stars. It's crucial to understand that when meeting with an agent, your job is basically to hand them theirs. The idea that an agent will figure out how to market or sell you is antiquated and vestige of times past (can you tell that my ghostwriter wrote that sentence?).

In comparison to when I started, right now there is so much more work, moving so much faster, in an environment that has become unbelievably more competitive. Unless you are working a shit-ton and making your agents bags of money, the odds of getting a sit down longer than forty- five minutes are basically zero. They are not interested in getting to know you, so from the very first minute of the meeting you need to be 'on'. You have to be an extraverted, shiny, version of your personality. Confidence is everything, and yet actors apologize more than most people I know. Auditioning in this business is brutal and agents are looking for clients who can compete in that arena. The shy wallflower who wasn't asked to dance will stay right where they are, on the wall and out of the audition room.

I want this book to be a wakeup call to actors who do not understand the business side of this industry. Agents only get paid when you work, so if you walk into the room and they're not seeing dollar signs because you're too busy pontificating about your craft or trying to show who you really are, chances are they're not going to sign you. This chapter is what agents aren't telling you.

BEING 'ON'

When meeting with an agent, confidence is key. It does not behoove you to walk in and apologize. When I was asked in a meeting, "What do you want to do?" I looked my agents directly in the eye and said, "I want to win an Academy Award." I didn't apologize. I didn't say, "I hope" or "I wish." I didn't say "maybe." I knew what I wanted. This isn't the time for self-deprecation. No matter who you are, no matter where you come from, you must walk into any room and be a star. This means you need to carry yourself with an inner light that radiates to everyone around you. Even if you are faking it . just fake it really, really well.

A student asked me, "What do I do when I'm meeting an agent?" Think of it like you're going on a first date or you are a guest on The Jimmy Kimmel Show. In either situation, you would want to portray the most magnificent version of yourself. You'd tell funny and engaging stories and be 'on.' Practice this skill. It will only help you as your career grows. What they want to see is confidence, not a person plagued by insecurity, doubtfulness or who is flaky. Nor do they want to see someone who is artsy-fartsy, wishy-washy, or out of touch with the business realities. When I walked into Kohner Agency they said, "What do you think you're better at, comedy or drama?" I replied, "Whatever you give me. That's what I'll be better at." The agents have to feel that you want it. Humility remains important, but fake modesty? No. Put it away. You have to show all of your strengths. Be a gladiator. A mistake many actors make is they go into meetings with all of the reasons why they won't be signed instead of all of the reasons why they will. Agents want to see one thing: confidence. Let me say that again. Confidence. Agents want to see a star.

Let me walk you through an example of where and how an actor can take a wrong turn in terms of how they're selling themselves, where they fail, and what I do to fix it. I worked with an actor who had a slight chip on his shoulder because he had been turned down by agents for several years.

Let's call him James. So, I jumped in and said, "Okay pretend I'm an agent. Tell me about yourself."

INT. STUDIO, DAY.

JAMES and SARA are sitting, conversing.

JAMES: Okay, well I'm from New York and have been in LA for about five years --

Sara interrupts him.

SARA: Let me stop you there. Say two. Because if you have been in LA for five years and you don't have an agent, I would start thinking, "what's wrong? You're older, why haven't you been able to get an agent?" And the second I start thinking like that, the chances of you being signed diminish quite quickly. So, think about tweaking the truth

Actors are way too honest when it comes to meetings but sadly not honest enough when it comes to the script .but that's something for another book. Agents lie all the time, and there are times when actors need to as well. So yes, I'm advocating that you lie. I'm not saying tis morally right, but everyone in Hollywood does it. I would also consider lying about your age. If you're twenty-nine and can pass for twenty-four, split the difference. If you're twenty-six, shave a few years off. Always say you are younger, and by the time you sign a contract with them, they will have forgotten. It is a youth obsessed industry, and taking a couple years off your age helps. Back to the story:

JAMES: I was working in NY as an actor.

SARA: What does that mean?

JAMES: I've been working in NY and Chicago solely as a stage actor, fully supporting myself financially, doing theater for like seven years.

SARA: That's amazing.

JAMES: Yeah, but agents won't care.

SARA: They won't care if you don't sell it. That's a huge asset and something to be proud of. It's about telling a story and how you spin it.

You're walking into an agent's office, thinking about all the reasons why they wouldn't sign you. So instead, spin it. Own it. Say something to the effect of "I could have been in LA a long time ago, but I was too busy doing off-Broadway theatre in New York. I've made a great living working in off-Broadway as well as touring the country and performing in reputable theatres." It's not that you're lying, you're just speaking a language that they can understand. You're taking a negative of "I've only worked in theatre" and spun it in a way that empowers you and makes you more marketable.

At this, James begins to perk up. He does not seem as defensive as before.

SARA CONT'D: What if I, a potential agent, were to ask about your in- room audition experience?

JAMES: (mumbling) It's not much. Although I was an in-room reader when they were casting Eight Mile.

SARA: Okay, that sounds good, tell me more about that.

As it turns out, when Eminem was in the room, he loved the work James was doing. He had James start running lines with him, and even asked if he'd be his on-set coach. While he was on set, both Mekhi Phifer and Eminem (along with other cast members) encouraged him to go to LA. Seven years later, he's working as a waiter and is ready to give up, because he "can't" get signed by an agent.

JAMES: What do I do?

SARA: Spin the story, but first, get rid of the chip on your shoulder. It makes you seem entitled and negative. It's a place that most actors visit way too often, and it's a quality that seeps into their work too frequently. If you have anger, resentment, or negativity, get rid of it. From this moment on, consider all of those qualities as kryptonite. You have a story, and it's a good one. It just takes some shifting.

I would suggest James say something to the effect of, "after supporting myself in theatre as a working actor, the casting director on Eight Mile asked if I would come in to be a reader. They needed someone good to read opposite the names that were coming in, and of course I said yes, because it's a phenomenal opportunity for any actor to be able to sit in a casting office and learn. While I was reading, Eminem loved the way I worked and asked me to come on set. While I was on set, I obviously learned a ton, and Mekhi (if you've worked with someone and have a relationship with them, use a first name only. You don't need to say Mekhi Phifer) was the one who said I should definitely come to LA.

You want to semi address the few years you've been here and why you haven't gotten an agent. Something along the lines of, "I didn't want to start looking for an agent immediately when I got to Los Angeles, because I wanted to make sure I knew how to audition. I know how talented I am, but stage auditions are different from film and TV. I studied intensively for a few months in preparation, so that when you, as my agent, send me into a room, I know you're going to get fantastic feedback."

Practice this version of your story. Practice it on dates. Practice it with family. Practice the art of telling your story. It's your job to know how to handle the brevity of an agent's attention span, and therefore how to master the beginning, middle, and end in a concise way that packs a punch.

A few weeks later he met with an agent, did the pitch, got signed, and has been a working actor ever since.

When I work with a performance coaching client, an athlete, an entertainer, an artist, or even someone in finance, early on in the work my question for them is always, "What is your biggest fear?" That's what I want you to start with before seeking an agent. What is your biggest fear? That you don't have enough credits? That you're too old? That you don't know how to market yourself? Or that they'll turn you down? Then I want you to figure out the response to that.

How can I spin my story in a way that they will have no choice but to sign me? If its age, start with that. If you address it as, "Look I know I'm old and starting late, but it's my passion", then agents will respect that you're mature enough to handle any truth. If it's that you don't have any credits, well what then can you offer? Can you speak another language? Do you have a list of wild special skills? Are you one-quarter Sioux? If you feel like you don't have anything to offer, then its not the right time to be looking for an agent. It's the time to be looking to find what you do have to bring to the table.

EMBRACING YOUR TYPE

You should know your type by now. If you don't, did you maybe just pick up the book and open it to a random page? Please don't do that. Go back to page one.

I am kidding, but it is startling to me how many actors are missing the mark in terms of knowing how they'll be cast. When traditional methods and methodology was developed, the training was based on learning how to become as many different types and different people / characters as possible. While that is classical training at its best, it does not serve today's film and TV actor. As I've mentioned, my method is about teaching my actors to become authentic versions of themselves instead of trying to act like something they are not. The hard part, I think, for most of you is marrying how you look in terms of society, Hollywood, the world, etc. with who you really are inside. Meaning you might feel like a dork, awkward in social situations and somewhat shy, but if you look like a super model, it's time to get with your badass inner self. The opposite is also true. If you look like a character actor, perhaps a Seth Rogan type, own that.

A manager I work with signed an actor because of his look (as do most agents in Hollywood, by the way). Eight months after being in Hollywood, he started going to extreme measures to lose weight, had his chin lipo'd, and was working to become a leading man. However, the manager had signed a

Seth Rogan type. A year or two later, the actor was asking me why he wasn't auditioning. I called his manager, and she told me flat out, "He's not the guy I signed. He was the funny, chubby, best friend or slacker, and now he's trying to be something he's not."

Embracing your type doesn't mean limiting yourself. It's something that actors struggle with and frequently ask other people to help them with. There are whole classes built on actors 'typing' each other. I personally just think it takes some common sense. A shortcut is to think in terms of high school. What club did you belong to? Were you the head cheerleader? Class clown? Were you in chess club? Do we all want to be the pretty, popular girl or the quarterback? Sure. But that's not who we all are, nor is it how we look.

If you look like Gabrielle Sidibe, don't say that you want to be doing Halle Berry roles. If you're 5'2" and 140 pounds, with an adorable, girl-next- door look, don't say that you want to do Angelina Jolie. Lena Dunham would have never been cast as the lead of her own show, let alone as a lead with the amount of nudity her role required, if she hadn't written, produced, and created the idea on her own. While typecasting is changing, Hollywood has a long way to go. Think in terms of stereotypes. On that note, actors need to stop saying "I don't want to be typecast". It's inevitable that you will be, and personally I think you should consider yourself lucky if you've gotten to the point in your career where you are type cast. When I got to Hollywood at 21, I was immediately was submitted for what were then called ingénue roles – young leading ladies I did an episode of Becker with Ted Danson, and the writers wanted to make me a series regular. When I came back to do a second episode, I had gone from a size six to a size eight, and suddenly my storyline changed. Wardrobe hinted that because of the weight gain – at most, ten pounds – they were no longer considering me for the show. It was now unbelievable for me to be a viable love interest for Ted, a man who is more than twenty years my senior.

Embracing your type is important, especially now that agents aren't helping us and expect the actor to come in knowing the kind of roles they are right for. As it is in acting, being specific is everything. If in your meeting, when asked about yourself, the answer is something like, "I'm a really good actor, am passionate about what I do, I love my craft, am easy to work with, and am an excellent communicator", you've made a mistake. This is a terrible pitch. Nobody cares if you're an excellent communicator, easy to work with, or are really sweet. An example of a great pitch might be for a twenty two year old, good looking, all American who says, "I see myself as the trust fund baby on CSI: NY who no one believes is a killer because of his innocent look, but of course at the end, we find out he's the one who raped and killed the girl. Also, I played football in high school and have been into athletics my who life, so I pretty much in any sports show I would feel comfortable playing an athlete. I also love the Modern Family style of comedy and could see myself as the perfect new boyfriend who has too much of a bromance with Phil."

Why is that a good pitch? In under a minute, you told this agent three different and very specific breakdowns they could submit you for today. It connects with how their brains work.

Meeting an agent or a manager is one of the most important steps in your career. Actors blow meetings with potential representation all the time. You have to go in and give them zero reason to not sign you. If you go in knowing yourself, knowing your product and knowing the business, then everyone sees the potential to make money. Why then, wouldn't an agent want to work with you?

Chapter 5

Class

The audition is the gate through which you must pass to be a working actor. Learn how to open the gate.

Let's talk about class. Actors are spending too much money on class. They are taking waaaay too many classes. In some ways, it's become a go-to for frustrated artists in this industry. When they complain to their agents, most of the time the answer they receive is either "take more class" or "get new headshots".

If it's not changing your life every single week, then it is time to find a new one. While I encourage every actor to study and understand Shakespeare, if you want to be working in front of the camera, then you need to be studying Sorkin, Shonda, and Scorsese. Go ahead and add to that list any notable screenwriter or showrunner who is working in film or TV today. Classes are focused way too much on traditional methodology. Some of the biggest 'guru' acting teachers in Los Angeles are continuing to teach methods that are not only outdated, but are also hurting actors. It's heartbreaking and frustrating on every level for me to see an actor at one of my intensives realize they've been paying a lot of money and wasting a lot of time on a class that just doesn't work. There are still quite a few teachers out there who believe they need to scream or yell or be borderline abusive in order to break an actor down. I think this is dangerous, stupid, totally unnecessary, and absolutely wrong in every way. The business beats us up enough. I consider my job to be empowering actors. I also believe that you don't have to spend years training. This idea is not conducive to today's world. We all have different hats we have to wear and jobs we have to do. Our training needs to be easier, less time consuming, and more effective. That was my mission in creating the Mornell Method. Find a teacher that challenges and, yes, scares you a little. You want your class to push you, you want to be inspired by your classmates, and you want to be getting up and working in every class. You should be able to take what you're learning in class and be able to apply it to your auditions and set experiences immediately. However, the most important aspect for actors to learn about this craft is the business of auditioning.

Auditioning is the hardest thing an actor has to do because the entire process is set up to make you fail. You get twelve pages of material at 7:00 P.M. for an appointment at 11:00 A.M. the very next day. This begins the process of clearing your schedule, or trying to get off work, or change a shift, or hire a babysitter, or find a classmate to work the material with. Hopefully you bust your ass to get phenomenal coaching (if needed), work to find unique choices, the right outfit, and race through traffic to get to the appointment on time. Then you sit and wait for sometimes over an hour while possibly seeing actors who are much more known than you, all while engaging in a constant battle against the voices in your head that are giving you all the reasons why you won't book this. You have to keep your focus and concentration while trying not to get pissed off about the fact that you're waiting. You go in with all three or four scenes prepared, only to have the casting director barely look up and say, "We're just doing scene two." Now you're fighting the part of your brain that wants to tell them to "fuck off" or that you'd "really like to do scene three, please."

Then, let's just say for example – scene two is where the love of your life is in an ocean, drowning, dying, and you have to say goodbye. How are you going to do that sitting on a chair with a casting director who won't look at you? How? Where's the water? Where's the love? Where's anything at all that would make it easier for you to act this scene? It's not there. And yet you need to pour out your heart and soul and make them believe. When you finish doing that, you're met with an insincere, "That was great, thank you," and a casting director who, by the way, still has not looked up, and you have to fight the urge to kill him or her. These are just the tip off the iceberg when it comes to ways that auditioning can be brutal.

My philosophy is that if auditioning is the hardest aspect of our career, why wasn't I taught at a school like Carnegie Mellon the actuality and reality of how to book a job? Because it isn't just about talent or ability. With the Mornell Method, isn't it my job to get actors on set? My job isn't to keep actors in class, it's to effectively and quickly teach actors what it takes to make phenomenal choices, to be prepared, and to be able to show up on set, hit their mark, say their lines in a believable wat that is honest and real to who they are. And yes, that process starts with the audition. The audition is not a safe space, nor is it a black box theatre where you have their undivided attention. It is just one of the hoops you have to jump through in order to secure a paycheck There are hundreds of thousands of amazing actors. Talented actors, who have never booked work because auditioning is just that hard. Even Lady Gaga, after her phenomenal performance in *A Star Is Born*, said that she started as an actress but couldn't handle auditioning and quit to become a singer. Thank God she is doing both.

While it is important to understand scene study, if you've spent years in a class learning what it is to break down, deconstruct, and rehearse in a scene, that process will fail you when it comes to being on set. The rehearsal on set consists of anywhere between two to five minutes of a director trying to figure out how to move you to make a scene work. Unless you are a lead on the show or film, directors are not going to be sitting down to discuss the scene and your characters beats, subtext, motivations, etcetera, etcetera, etcetera. Most of the time they are asking for you to move, hit your mark, and say your line in a believable way. Don't just go and try a bunch of classes. My suggestion would be to audit some classes and get very specific about what it is that you want to learn. If class is taught by someone who hasn't worked on a set in over a decade or just has a few credits on their resume, or is still teaching classical methods, my suggestion would be to save your money and put it towards cable, HBO, Netflix, Showtime, and use your time analyzing and studying film and TV with a group of friends instead of paying someone to "break you down" in a three hour Meisner class. You cannot use Meisner in an audition. You cannot sit there and repeat back with a casting director. And you certainly cannot do the scene with them because, news flash, they're not acting with you. That is not their job. They are not actors, they are casting. Their job is to judge and observe what your choices are and what you would bring to the role. Actors say all the time that they tried to connect with the casting director, and that is a mistake. The art form of auditioning goes against everything that actors learn in school or conservatory training. Auditioning is an art form to actors and a business to casting directors, and those differing viewpoints are incredibly difficult to reconcile. Actors need to get better at understanding the business side of auditioning, because casting sure as hell isn't going to make an effort to understand the art side.

Take an audition class, or improv, or comedy, just be sure that it is current If you are in a comedy class that is teaching you multi-cam technique that worked in the 70s and 80s, it is not current. Not only is it unhelpful, it can be destructive to an actor's career. Find a class that is going to give you the skills required to book the job.

Find a teacher who scares you and challenges you. You can get any one of your friends to say that you should try it faster, slower, bigger, or smaller, but what you want in a coach is someone who knows you, your strengths and what you can bring into the room, but will also going to push the hell out of you. That being said, let me address the method of teaching that so many are still using (and needs to be eradicated, in my opinion). I'm speaking of the semi-abusive, 'let me tear you down in order to build you up' type. STAY AWAY FROM THOSE TEACHERS. RUN. The business will beat you up enough, if your coach isn't strengthening and empowering you while being honest, then it is time to find a new coach. It's not so much about studying their method, but more about learning what works for you and how you can authentically bring yourself to the work.

CHAPTER 6

Before The Audition

*Don't panic. Take note these steps and you'll be fine.
Ignore them and you might get fucked.*

Ninety eight percent of booking a job is out of your hands. Let's stop, pause, and read that sentence again. Ninety eight percent of booking a job is out of your hands. This is unlike any other profession in the world, where if you work hard and are the best person for the job, it ultimately pays off.

Casting now has become a decision by committee. There are a huge number of variables that go into how and why one particular actor books the job over another actor. This chapter is about mastering the two percent that you can control. While this won't be an in-depth description of the Mornell Method or how to prepare an audition, it will address some of the most common questions that have been confusing actors for decades. Questions that all start when you first get the appointment or CMail.

ASSESS THE SITUATION

Read the entire appointment sheet and all of the information. I realize that sounds ridiculously simple, but you would be shocked and stunned at how many actors bypass this part and miss pertinent information. When is it due? Are they asking for all scenes or are they telling you to pick one? Is this a self-tape or in-room? I could go on and on, and the fact that I even need to write this is frustrating. Still, it is so often an issue for most of the actors that come into our studio that it is borderline an epidemic. Read all the information. Go slowly. Make sure you understand everything that is being asked of you.

MAKE YOUR AGENTS JOB EASIER

Confirm right away. If your phone doesn't have email alerts set up, then do that immediately. Literally, put this book down right now and activate your email alerts right now. I'm not joking. Confirm without questions. In this day and age, actors need to work harder at being self-sufficient. If it is for a series regular and they don't include the script, you can always ask if there is one available. Other than that, your email response, which should be within an hour of getting the appointment, should be "thank you, confirmed"

MANAGE YOUR TIME

Think of yourself more like an athlete training for a competition than an actor preparing for an audition. The reality (and what I teach) is that an actor should be able to prepare for any audition in under two to three hours. If you need two days with the material, then you are in the wrong class. How much time do you need to prepare? Do you need to get a babysitter or get a shift covered? My suggestion when working with difficult material is to grab a partner, rehearse, work the scene, and hit the trail when possible. Just walking around the block will work miracles for actually learning the material instead of just memorizing it.

DECIDE IF YOU NEED TO COACH

Remember that a phenomenal coach takes what you are doing and elevates it to the next level. If you aren't getting that out of a session, then work to find a coach who can do that with you. It isn't their audition; it's about taking your instincts and directing you in a way that is both personal and solidifies confidence in your choices.

NO

Get familiar with using the word, "No." "No, I can't drive you to the airport, I have an audition." "No, I can't feed your cat, I have an audition." "No, I can't be your tour guide right now, even though you just flew 3,000 miles to see me. I have an audition." "No, I can't come to your birthday party, I just got an audition." For me, showing up absolutely prepared and doing the best job I can takes every single minute that I have. Most of the time, you're not going to get more than a day to prepare. That's the rule, not the exception.

REHEARSE.

This sounds, again, totally obvious, and yet most actors who take my audition intensive have no idea how to prepare. My suggestion is to rehearse fully. To make it look effortless in the room, you need to prep like a dancer or athlete, not like an actor who is afraid to "get in their head". To make it truly effortless, you need to do it one thousand times. Actors tell me all the time that they are afraid of 'over rehearsing'. I don't believe in the concept of being over-rehearsed. My only caveat is that if you are working with deeply emotional material, hold the actual emotion until you get in the room. Don't 'test' it. In terms of the technical aspects of the audition, rehearse, rehearse, rehearse.

It's not about running the lines; it's about working the scene. If the scene is in a car, do it in your car while you're driving. Christina Ochoa and I did this before her audition for *Blood Drive*, and with every callback, she would return to and keep rehearsing in her car until she booked it. If you're a chef, rehearse in the kitchen while cooking. You cannot fake what you haven't felt, and instead of working through imagination, I urge you to pull from experience.

Get creative in your rehearsal. One example that I like to share is LaMonica Garrett's audition for *Designated Survivor*. It was a frantic scene where the world was blowing up and the President is missing, and his character has to run in and tell Kiefer Sutherland that he is now the acting President of the United States. Lots of action, high stakes, very dramatic. The way we prepped (short of killing the President) was to work the scene while playing Go Fish. It helped him so much that he took one of the Jokers from the deck and still carries it with him to this day. Multitasking, doing things like playing cards while working dialogue, is one of the most beneficial things an actor can do for their preparation. And no offense to the men who I work with, but multitasking is often not in your DNA. It might be hard and you might hate it, but it will strengthen your in-room auditions.

CHOOSE AN OUTFIT.

Unless it's a commercial audition, you never want to bash them over the head with your wardrobe choices. If it's a period piece, dress with a 'suggestion' of the character, period or genre. Also, if it is an existing show, watch it and pay attention to the wardrobe. For example, *The Walking Dead* tends to lean on dark blues, browns, greens, and grey. Do everything you can to help the casting directors recognize how you would fit within the show.

One of the reasons why I booked a recurring role as Ted Danson's neighbor on Becker was because of my wardrobe choices. My character, Anita, was supposed to be a high-priced escort, something which Ted Danson's *Becker* did not recognize. I was the only actor at the audition who showed up in jeans and a sweatshirt. Everyone else looked like – well – hooker.

I suggest having a few go-to audition outfits. Anything to save you from that dreaded last-minute scramble. Consider what roles you go in for and have an outfit for each. Don't go for what you think is right versus wrong; instead make a choice based on fact and research, and then bring your own sense of style and finesse to that. If you are going out for the lead of a show, you need to walk in looking like you're ready to go straight onto set. Ladies if you're tall, I suggest you invest in some really great flats. Gentlemen, I suggest you find a versatile pair of work boots that would work for military / police / or laborer. Plus, a nice pair of boots can look incredibly sexy on guys.

Side Note: Shoes tell a lot about a person. When I look around a waiting room, I can tell who's been working and who's been struggling. More importantly than that, shoes literally give us the foundation and the feel of who we are playing from the ground up. I worked with an actor who was, let's say 'vertically challenged'. In his day to day life, his go-to look was always cowboy boots. Once he was coaching for a David E. Kelley pilot, and he was wearing penny loafers. Everything about how he moved and walked was smaller. I told him, "before you go in the room, go home and get your cowboy boots." He responded doubtfully, saying that he was reading for a teacher. I said, "I don't care. You're going to look, better, feel better, and move better with them. More importantly, you're going to walk into the room with confidence if you wear those boots. You should wear them to every audition you go into". He booked that job and has been working nonstop ever since.

BE ON TIME

Arrive ten to fifteen minutes before your audition. Some actors tell me they like to get to the audition thirty minutes early, but that's going to piss some casting directors off. "I was late because of traffic" absolutely is not acceptable. There's a story about Lea Michele getting into an accident on her way to her callback for Glee. She was literally pulling glass out of her hair, but she got there like a pro.

HEADSHOT AND RESUME

At a certain point in your career, you get to stop taking them with you. Until then, unless specified or told not to, you should always carry a current headshot and resume with you.

FILM IT YOURSELF FIRST

If you really want to know what your audition is going to look like, and considering that most actors should have their own home set up for self- tapes, there is no harm to setting up your camera and watching it back. It's going to be the most accurate measure of what you're going to do in the room. If something doesn't work on the tape, it's going to be obvious and you can change it. This is one of those extra steps that few actors take but can be a real game changer.

CHAPTER 7

Addressing The Room

This is about demystifying the audition room. These are the top reasons i hear actors say, "i bombed my audition," and how to fix it, unless you're just a shitty actor.

When it comes to auditioning, actors have one thing in common: no one really does it well. Actors go into the room with uncertainty and doubt, and it kills their chance of booking. This is true across the board, whether it's a new actor, graduate of a Yale program, or someone who's just come off a successful series. When I started working with Rose Rollins, she had just come of the *L Word* and was back to auditioning. Not only was she hating the process, she wasn't booking and it was starting to get into her head. "What top three things are bothering you the most in terms of auditioning?", I asked her when we first met. Her response was, "The waiting room. I don't like sitting there and dealing with all the other actors. Secondly, the way we are treated. It is never a comfortable space and I get uncomfortable. And third, of course, is the reader. The fact that they don't give anything or read too slow or too fast... it really feels like I have nothing to act off of." So, I told her we were going to change all of that right now. This is what she sent me after that first session:

Sara, I want you to know my time with you yesterday turned everything around for me today. I had my headphones on, listening to music outside the room which kept me focused. I felt grounded and truthful in my feelings. I had control and felt really good about my read in the room.

No matter what stage of the game you're at, these tips can hopefully help you give yourself permission to protect and prepare yourself for the reality of the room.

There are so many myths and misconceptions about auditioning because classes are being taught by people who have either never auditioned or auditioned thirty years ago. If I were to take a decade's worth of audition-related questions (and believe me, there have been hundreds if not thousands of them of them), they would boil down to these. ALL of them can be avoided. Most people just haven't been taught how. I see a lot of actors beat themselves up when I give them answers that seem so glaringly obvious. In return, what I say to them is, "Do you speak French? If not, how could you expect to understand me if I started speaking French? You have to learn it." Auditioning is an art form in and of itself and a completely different language than acting.

Mastering the technicality of the audition is absolutely vital. Going into the room with any technical questions in the front or back of your mind results in uncertainty and doubt. Those two things will absolutely kill the chance of booking. Knowing how to master the technicality of auditioning will take the guesswork out of what to do or not do in the audition room.

1. IT'S A GLADIATOR'S ARENA, NOT A SAFE SPACE

The casting director didn't even look at me, and they didn't even have a chair.

Too many actors are going into the room like lambs to slaughter. I think this is emblematic of the safe space mentality in acting classes set in a black box theatre. The fact is there will either be a chair or there won't be. Rehearse both ways. Often, you can walk into a room and have the assistant acknowledge you, but the casting director will be preoccupied on her phone or computer. It's a horrible feeling to prepare, to train, to move a shift, to pay for coaching, to do everything in your power to get there, only to walk in and not be acknowledged as a human being. That fucks with our psyche. What I suggest is be aware of the energy in the room; work on shielding yourself from it instead of being affected by it. The subtle shift I encourage is to think about walking into the audition room 'on' as opposed to 'open'.

2. THE WAIT.

They kept me waiting for over an hour, so when I went in the room, I was just so frustrated and angry.

This is again something that affects us on a cellular level. We are not being paid to audition. As a matter of fact, at this point most actors are paying an enormous amount just to get to the point where they have an audition and are getting into rooms. To sign in and see an hour or two-hour wait is totally disrespectful and, in my opinion, heinously wrong in terms of respecting our time. That being said, there is the reality of the wait. How you handle that is a choice. If sitting with twenty actors for an hour is going to mess with your head, then find out who signed in ahead of you, and take a walk around the block.

One of our job requirements is patience. I personally battled with that most of my career, and to this day, I still do. When I worked to get there on time and prepared for the role only to see casting be running an hour behind, part of me would get really frustrated. I'm aware of that voice, and when I start to get frustrated, I need to take a walk or leave. This is because I know if I walk into the room with that voice, the one that is pissed because you've devalued my time, I'm not going to do my best work. If you are going to go into the room angry and it doesn't work for the character, then your audition is going to be off and it will not be worth it. This is a career of hurry up and wait, with an emphasis on the wait. If you're going to be bothered by the fact that you're going to have to wait, I would strongly advise looking into other professions. Become a doctor or airline pilot and make other people wait for you.

Side Note: Like every rule, there are exceptions. A student of mine was a reader during pilot season. Casting was running two hours late and down to their last two guys. First actor comes in and the executive producer apologizes for keeping him waiting. "Hey man, that's totally cool, I get it," says the actor, "It's pilot season, no big deal." After finishing his audition, he thanked the room a couple times for bringing him in. The last actor comes in, executive producer again apologizes for keeping him waiting, and the actor responds, "You fucking should be sorry. It's pilot season and I've got a ton of other appointments. Now let's read this and hope it's fucking funny." He finished his read and without a word, walked out of the room. Guess who got the callback? Mr. Took-Control-of-the-Room.

3. MUSIC IS YOUR FRIEND.

I got caught up in conversation with a friend I hadn't seen in a while and then was thrown because I could hear everyone else's audition before me. Actors tell me all the time that they get "distracted" by everyone in the waiting room, or that they get thrown by hearing everyone else's audition. There's a really simple solution to all of this. Have headphones with you in the waiting room. For me, music is everything, it is crucial. Not only is it your deterrent of distractions, but it also helps me keep my energy where it needs to be for the role. If my character just found out her husband died, then I listen to songs that create an emotional vulnerability in me. If I'm going in for a half hour comedy or something lighter, then I am listing to something peppy or makes me feel upbeat. Music helps me create a direct line to what my character is thinking and feeling. It also keeps me focused on the arena, not the distractions.

4. 90% IN CHARACTER.

Do I walk into the room as the character?

A big question I'm asked is, "should I walk into the room 'in character'". The answer is yes. They are no longer looking for an actor to come into the room and transform into the character, they are looking for the person who is the role to walk into the room. The people who are hiring us are not creative professionals. You want to bring the version of yourself that energy-wise, look-wise, feel-wise, is the character. Don't break away from that version of yourself until several episodes into shooting, if ever. I've seen actors shoot themselves in the foot because they are auditioning to play a sexy, badass, tough, strong, gorgeous superhero, but when they walk into the room, they revert back to their quiet, introverted, and even a bit dorky personality. That will confuse executive producers who are looking for the inside to perfectly match the outside.

If your character is devastated, don't walk into the room perky, or feeling like you need to show them that you are "easy to work with". If the scene, for example, is about a girl who just lost a parent, but you walk into the room with a lightness, you are taking away from the creditability of your performance. Truthfully, they are most likely already dismissing you in their minds. They should want to cast you from the second that you walk into the room. They won't be able to follow a one-hundred-and-eighty-degree turn; if you go in peppy with a Susy Sunshine attitude, but your character is in a darker place, then trust me, they are already thinking about the next actor.

This is also about protecting you. Glenn Close may be able to turn it on and off instantaneously, but that is a skill that takes decades to hone. The work is to be truthful and honest in the material, and keeping yourself energetically in the same place as your character will only make the acting less evident (which, by the way is the goal). Respect and honor where you need to be as the character.

PROPS. MIMING...DON'T.

In the audition, my character is supposed to be holding a gun, but I had no idea what to use.

What I tell my actors is that auditions have set us up to fail. How many times have you said to yourself, "it would be so much easier if I was just filming this on set"? When we are auditioning, we are having to compensate for the fact that we aren't supported in ANY way. No lighting, no set, no props, and no other actors. Auditioning is acting alone, which goes against the foundation of any great acting training.

When you mime, it comes across as theatrical, and it is going to confuse the network or studio executive who is making the final decision on who they hire for the job. If you're supposed to be drinking a cup of coffee and you mime that, it is not only going to look ridiculous and like you're on stage, but it's going to make you feel like an asshole. We don't mime when we're shooting, unless the scene is making fun of actors. If you're drinking a cup of coffee in a scene, have a cup of coffee. I did a pilot for HBO called Kilroy. It was created, written, and produced by George Clooney and his team. In my audition scene, my character enters to meet her boyfriend at a Starbucks, and the first thing I do is grab the cup of coffee he brought to me, drink it, and then react to the fact that he hadn't put any Equal in it. I was working part time as a nursery school teacher and so beyond broke that coming up with the $1.50 for a cup of coffee was a big deal. However, I was absolutely not going to go into that room and mime drinking coffee. No way in hell. I made time to stop, buy, and have a real cup of coffee that I used in the room. And yes, I booked the job. Having something real, e.g. unsweetened black coffee to react to, takes away the need to act.

What if the scene calls for a gun? Holding my hand like it's a gun always feels a little bit weird. In general, miming makes me feel like an asshole. Anything that makes me feel increasingly fake in an already fake environment takes me out of the audition. There are so many simple and creative solutions that can keep an actor more connected to what they're doing than miming. I've had working actors go in-room and use their kids toy gun. I've used my phone and I've folded my sides in a way that I can use. It isn't necessarily about what you're using, but more how real you are treating whatever you are substituting for the actual prop.

More and more now, casting directors are sending out notes in all caps stating 'NO PROPS ALLOWED'. This is hurting and trapping actors. It pertains to those who are using props to the point of distraction. A prop should never take away from the audition. I've been incredibly creative with having and using a "prop" in an audition. For example, when coaching on Star Wars, actors work with dummy sides, and the scenes tend to be very conversational. Conversational is not an adjective I would use to describe Star Wars, and the trap becomes walking in and not having an action, activity, or prop, which inevitably makes the scene too focused on dialogue. A simple yet highly effective solution is taking a paper-clip and using it throughout the scene as if you are defusing a bomb, or putting together wires, etc. It doesn't take much to bring the audition to life. Having a paper clip, tennis ball, or rubber band just to give yourself some action can help keep your audition grounded, real, and conversational instead of presentational and theatrical. Bottom line: if it would be on your person or in your purse, use it. And never mime unless asked.

DON'T SHAKE.

The casting director wouldn't shake my hand!

Actors will say to me, "When I went to shake a casting director's hand, he looked at me like I was a leper". If they're seeing 200 actors and they shake everyone's hand, the chances of them getting sick is pretty high. Just don't do it.

SCAN THE ROOM

It was such a small room that I was thrown because the producer was practically in my lap, so I ended up not facing towards the camera for part of my audition!

The number one thing an actor needs going into the room is confidence. This is a tricky one because when you walk into an unfamiliar room, you automatically feel at a disadvantage. When I walk in, I do my best Terminator-like scan of the room. I'm immediately assessing where everything is placed and who is sitting in what position. The first thing I locate is the reader. That dictates where I'll be auditioning, always across from them. Find the camera and make sure your body is angled towards the camera. If there are producers in the room, acknowledge them. Don't eye-fuck each and every one of them, just say hello to the group in general. Be courteous, get to your mark, and get ready to begin your audition. Your command of the room and of the audition begins the second you walk in the door.

SITTING VS STANDING

Well, I'd rehearsed it sitting, but when I got into the room, there wasn't a chair.

Rehearse your scenes both sitting and standing. Let me repeat this again for the people in the back. Rehearse your scenes both sitting and standing! If you rehearse both ways and can do either, you will never be thrown for a loop. Know which one you prefer, so if they ask which you prefer, there is no hesitation. Physically you should also know how your character will sit or stand. If I'm playing a cop and I sit down and cross my legs, I feel 'out of it' immediately. Part of my rehearsal is spent determining how this person or character or professional sits, stands, and moves, and then working to use that to support the choices I've made.

DON'T BE AFFECTED BY THE ENERGY OF THE ROOM

When I walked in, I already knew they didn't like me.

Don't let yourself be affected by negative energy or distractions. Prepare to wait for a long time, be treated like crap and for them to ignore you and rush you through the process. If that doesn't happen, let it be a lovely surprise. Plan for someone's cell phone to go off. Distractions are a reality of our job. When you are working material before your audition, make sure you practice with distractions. You should be able to act through an earthquake.

I once auditioned for the role of a psychologist. In the waiting room, I watched several actresses leave the room flustered. When I got into the tiny room, the casting director was rushed, tense, and disorganized. Without looking at me, she demanded, "Do you have a picture and a resume?" I smiled at her and said, "No, I don't carry those anymore." Once you hit a certain level in your career, you no longer need to carry headshots. She proceeded to try and make me feel bad. "Well, okay then. Fine.", she huffed, "I'll just look you up on IMDb." The more frenzied and angrier she got, the calmer I became. When she got to the camera and asked if I had any questions, my response was simple, "Both my parents were shrinks. I've got this."

After we finished, she burst out, "Oh my god, I just feel like I actually went through therapy." I smiled, said, "Of course you did.", and stood up to walk out. As I walked to the door, she gasped, dropped to the floor, and started touching my leopard print boots (once again, see the importance of good shoes). From the ground she professed a deep love for my shoes. And in that moment, as I was looking down at this casting director literally on her knees, I knew I had won.

Five minutes previous, I had walked in on her determined to be a cunt. If I had apologized or weakened myself in any way, then she would have jumped on me like a lion on a gazelle. I held my own, was firm and professional, and refused to let her diminish me. By staying in my strength, she backed down to the point where she was on the floor petting and praising my boots.

It also helps that I was very fucking prepared. I wasn't there to make friends, and neither should you be. You are there to protect yourself and give a phenomenal performance.

SCREWING UP THE SCREW UP.

The casting director started before I was ready, so I was off and I flubbed my lines. But I just kept going.

There's nothing worse than seeing an actor flub a line or lose his place in the script and try to power through it anyway. Sherry Thomas of Bialy/Thomas Casting taught me this lesson. I was auditioning for *Better Call Saul,* and halfway through it I got in my head, and stumbled over a line. I stopped myself and said, "let me take that again." Sherry's response was not one of condemnation, which I think is something many actors fear, but of relief.

Her actual words were, "I fucking love that you do that Sara. I love that you stop yourself. I call actors in who I want to see. I want to see their choices. But it is really rough to watch them realize they've flubbed and insist on struggling through it. Refusing to stop is not admirable. It wastes my time because I have to send a perfect take." On set you may stop, call for a line, and keep going to not stop the take; auditioning is a different beast.

Actors think it's the end of the world if their performance wasn't perfect or that making a mistake is a fuck up. Sometimes it is the flubs, the imperfections that make your audition unique and true to life. The mistakes can be golden. However, if I mess up a line and I can't sell it or make it work, I will stop and say, "let me take that again." I don't apologize. What we do is hard. Remember that. You have nothing to apologize for. If you need to stop and start again, don't say sorry, just do it. What they will see is an actor who knows what they need to do in order to give them a perfect take.

BE FEARLESS IN BEING YOU.

I'm just not sure what they want and the breakdown isn't really me.

A few years after *Training Day*, I got the opportunity to work with Antoine Fuqua, who was then directing a pilot for FOX. In one of my scenes, my character was supposed to be giving a toast at a dinner party. They had me in very high stilettos and the set was freezing cold, so my feet were numb.

When I stood to give the toast, mid-sentence, I wobbled and stumbled. Mid-take, I looked right into camera and said, "Sorry, whoops." In front of 200 people, he yells, "Cut!" and as he walking towards me, he launched into a tirade, "You never stop take. That would've been perfect. You could've sold that you were slightly tipsy which would've worked for the character and worked for the scene." He actually said "You can stop a take in an audition, but not when you're on set. That is the director's job."

By this point in the day, I had felt bullied by him in several scenes and his 'don't fuck this up or the pilot will suck' direction. Instead of cowering while he berated me, I shot back, "Maybe you should have real wine in these glasses instead of grape juice." By standing up for myself, I was able to break the tension and he started laughing. He agreed, "Maybe you're right.", and then we had a nice conversation about the wine merchant on Santa Monica Boulevard. What Anton told me is a lesson I pass along whenever possible. He said, "Sara, the reason why I cast you was because you were the only actress in your audition who was working to fight the emotion, who was working to stay strong. All the other actresses were just trying to cry and be sad. I hired you because of your strength, and then in my direction I tried to take that away from you earlier today. That is wrong, and it is my fault, because your strength is what defines you. It is what separates you from the other actresses we saw. It is an innate part of you, and don't let anyone try to take that away from you."

Actors are beaten, beaten by rejection, beaten by coaches, and beaten by managers. We are told we are not enough or not right or should be somebody other than our true selves. Despite this, what books a role is having the courage and honesty to come from a place that is real for you, some place that is unique to you. The worst thing an actor can try and do is be someone else. This is ironic, considering that the majority of our training has been based in teaching us how to act like other people. If you don't believe me, remember the words of Antoine Fuqua, "who you are separates you from the masses." Trust that, hone that, be fearless in it, and you will start to see a shift in your callback and booking rate.

LEAVE

After I finished my audition, I didn't know what to do, so I asked, "Do you need to see something different? Should I do it again?"

I want actors to stop handing control over. That applies across the board, but particularly so when it comes to the audition room. Every room is different, and that makes this incredibly challenging. However, you know there will always either be a chair, or there won't. There will always either be a camera, or there won't. There will always be someone reading badly, or someone reading only sort-of-badly. You know the room is set up to make us fail. I want you to walk into the room and take control of your own audition. Get in, get to the work, and get out. Know how you're going to start, and know how you're going to finish. Start strong and finish even stronger. After you finish the audition, if you deflate, or ask them if they need more, or wait for them to dismiss you, you are not in control. They are. Remember that you are the only one not getting paid. Once you finish your take, take a moment of eye contact and simply say, "Thank you for bringing me in.", and move to leave. They will either start a dialogue or say "Thank you for coming in." If the latter occurs, don't gush. To be overly grateful just seems disingenuous and weird. You have been the one paying through class, countless hours of rehearsal, gas, Ubers, and parking. Simply say thank you, smile and leave. If they change their mind or want to see something different, they will chase you down. Let them, because it feels really good if they do.

CHAPTER 8

Self Tapes

We need to change our attitude from "I hate self taping" to "my self tape was fucking incredible".

As I've stated before, auditions are basically set up to make us fail. I have no idea when or why the audition process became such a shit show, for lack of better words. With the rise of the self-tape, actors finally have the opportunity to control how they do their auditions. So many actors complain and hate having to self-tape; to be perfectly honest, this baffles me. Antiquated training is conditioning actors to think that the audition room is going to be some sort of kumbaya, embracing, warm situation, but the opposite is true.

Auditioning is literally the opposite to the foundation of what HAS BEEN theatrical training. There were so many times in LA where I would be coaching a client and we would get to a point where the material was magic. The chemistry between us and the effortlessness of being both honest and in the moment made it was the kind of work we all aspire to do. Countless times we'd look at each other, be it someone with only a few credits or someone established like Jesse Williams or Rose Rollins, and say, "If only we could do this in the room!"

Now, with the rise of self-tapes (and that's something that won't go away) we are going to see more and more actors without massive credits booking films and television shows not because of training and technique, but because they are the role. Executes do not want to hire actors anymore; they want to hire the actual person. When it comes to self-tapes, we need to learn how to set ourselves up for success.

DON'T BE CHEAP

Stop being cheap. Just stop it. It is one of the biggest downfalls for an actor. In Atlanta, it has become a joke when we see actors on Facebook starting a discussion about the best studio to tape at or use the excuse that someone's (mine) prices are too high. There is an acceptance of mediocrity, and while that may be fine with some people, to truly succeed in this industry I strongly urge you to demand excellence from not only yourself, but from your training and those around you.

When it comes to taping, invest in the quality. It is an investment in yourself and your work. Find a studio with someone you can work off of, instead of someone who is acting like a casting director or reader in an audition room. What is the point of paying for a service that is running their self-tapes like a casting office? It doesn't make sense to me. You have control over lighting, sound, how it's being shot, everything. This is your audition. Don't let someone else dictate what it should be.

GET A READER

The biggest thing that has changed as a result of self-tapes is that now agents and managers can see our work. After years of the audition being somewhat secretive and a mystery, it is now out there, online, available for people to see, judge, and critique. Actors who, previously, may have been with an agency for years might now only last a few months if the agents don't like the quality of work that the actor is doing. Instead of just relying on the casting directors' feedback, agents and managers are now starting to weigh in on our work. They send tapes to me when they are not happy with the work, but can't really explain to a client why that's true or how they should change it.

One of the first things I will notice that is 90% of the time atrocious are the people reading off camera. Find a better reader, and by that, I mean a much, much better reader. Your mom / boyfriend / cousin / whomever should only step in when there is an emergency or you are out of the country. I tell my actors to get better at rehearsing and finding someone you love reading with. Getting a better reader or a partner who you work with well, who gives you enough to work off of without overdoing it, is one of the most valuable investments an actor can make or find for themselves. Having a bad reader or someone who is reading like a casting director takes away from the quality of the tape and from the actor's performance.

PROPS

We get not in massive bold letters NO PROPS! NO PROPS! I totally disagree with this and think it's another way that actors are being set up to fail. Miming not only kills auditions but also confuses network executives. Miming is theatrical and our auditions should be anything but that. We should be working to be cinematic, not theatrical.

My rule for props is as follows: use them and get creative with them. If it says she's smoking, you don't necessarily need to smoke. Chew gum so long as it isn't distracting. For a show I was working on, I made a choice to chew tums Instead of smoking cigarettes because it seemed like something that would work for a detective. For many of the dummy-sided Star Wars auditions I've worked on, we've had to be incredibly creative to keep the actors active. I've had actors use everything from a paperclip to a magazine to a baseball to a Rubik's Cube to a thousand other things that have been embraced and loved by casting.

A prop should work with you to keep a scene natural, grounded, conversational, and real. If the focus becomes solely on dialogue with no action (meaning no props of any kind) then no matter what the material or quality of the work, it will appear theatrical and overdone. It doesn't take much. Something as small as twirling a rubber band between two fingers can immediately bring the scene down and take acting out of the equation. Unless it is a soap opera or Tyler Perry, acting needs to stay out of the equation. Using a prop that doesn't take away from your performance or distract the viewer will separate your tape from the hundreds of other tapes casting directors are watching. The people who are hiring us are non-creative and somewhat literal. It can be hard for them to imagine the scene with movement or how it would be shot if the actor is doing it without any props, movement, or action. We need to tailor the audition to work for the minds of the people who are hiring us.

KNOW THE SHOW

Just like your work, your tapes need to be specific. It is why I encourage you to watch tv as much as possible. This bears fruit when it comes to taping because you should be tailoring your self-tapes to the film or show for which you are auditioning. When my friend Salli Richardson directs, she studies the show to see what they have already captured, what their style, pace, feel, lighting, and look are. She isn't coming in as a director trying to put her stamp on the show; she looks at what has already been created and works to follow that model. Actors should be doing the same when they audition. Your wardrobe, the camera setup, and the lighting should be a mini reflection of the show or film they are for. Within reason of course. Don't go too far, as you don't want to beat them over the head with it. A few good examples of this are the early Game of Thrones auditions. Although the show hadn't come out yet, the actors are still tailoring their tapes to work for them, the network, and the roles they are auditioning for. If it is a pilot or a show that hasn't come out yet, you're going to have to make an educated guess. If its HBO, it should be grounded, real, and darker. If its network, it will be brighter and more formulaic. Your job is not to reinvent the wheel or put your own spin on an existing show, it is to exist within the confines of what has already been created.

EDITING

If you haven't edited your own self-tapes or sat in while someone else does it, I highly suggest that you try. It is really important for you to see what works and what doesn't on camera. Watching your own tapes with a critical lens and seeing what is effective, as well as how this impacts editing, is an invaluable skill for any actor. Additionally, when you do go in room, casting directors don't have time to edit tapes. You have to give them what I call a 'cut, print, moving on' take. Your audition should be reflective of a close up on set rather than a master shot. It should be easy for them to cut and your opening beat should be clean. The entire performance has to be camera friendly. If you aren't sure what that means, it's another reason for you to sit in the editing room. The camera is a fickle beast, the best way to learn is to sit in the editing bay.

OPENING MOMENTS

Think of your opening moment as being more akin to a photograph than a backstory, subtext, or thought. It has to look good. The same thing applies to your end frame. It should be clean and neat. Soap holds (looking at the reader until the camera cuts), exiting frame, or returning to any action you were doing at the top the scene all work well.

Actors are doing way too much. Way, way too much. If, for example, you are going in for a one-line waitress role with the line "Can I take your order?", your opening frame could be you looking at your notepad while taking a step into frame, then looking up at your reader and asking to take their order. If they respond, "We need a minute.", go back to looking at your notepad as you clear frame. Your opening moment isn't about you being exhausted, tired, and ready to end your shift; it's about having an action and opening frame that, when a network executive or producer looks at your tape, reads 'waitress'. An action, not subtext, will do this. Having a clear action at the start of a scene and then going back to that at the end of the scene puts a nice bow on the audition and makes it easier for them to hire you.

SIZE OF THE ROLE

Be aware of the size of the role. The choices you make and the way you should approach a costar, recurring costar, guest start, recurring guest star, recurring or series regular are all different. When you are going in for a supporting, no name, one line, or one day guest, it is not about you. You are literally supporting the lead. Stop making it about your own choice or character, and make it about the other people in the scenes with you.

The first role I ever booked was a waitress with the line, "Can I get you some coffee?" The directors feedback watching my tape after about twenty others was, "Her. She's the only one I believe was actually a waitress." I knew the line wasn't about me, but about moving the story along. There is an art form to 'just saying the line'. Those kinds of roles should look effortless. Absolutely effortless. If you feel like you are working too hard in the scene, you haven't rehearsed enough for it to become second nature. By the time you finished with most supporting roles, it should feel as if you did absolutely nothing. That is the sweet spot. For guest stars, be aware of the formula of the show. For series regulars, in general take more risks. When it comes to breaking down more material for bigger roles . . . well that's another book (that is hopefully coming soon).

BE METICULOUS

Be meticulous and proud of the work you are doing. Stop trying to get it 'right'. It is not about right or wrong, but about common sense, educated guesses, and bringing yourself to the role. This is a competition and you are competing against hundreds if not thousands of others. Raise the bar on yourself and on your work. Know that this is a numbers game; the better your tapes, the more auditions you are going to get, and the more offices are going to call you in. Casting is looking for quality. Take pride and be sure that the tape you send in will be one of the five best that they see.

CHAPTER 9
Atlanta

If you think that Atlanta has bad traffic. Just trust me. It doesn't.

In 2016, I made the decision to relocate to Atlanta with the somewhat ambitious goal of building a film and TV studio that would be attached to a two-year conservatory program. The idea was to build a place where actors come and get real life training while also providing opportunities behind the camera for a community of like-minded people. Our mission is to build a studio with a focus on female driven content, female driven directors, female driven crew, female driven .well, everything.

When I first started doing intensives, I chose to come to Atlanta. The impetus for creating a two-day intensive program focusing on the reality of auditioning came from the epidemic of casting director workshops. At this point, I had been training actors at a very high level in private for years, and had very rarely worked with beginners (this only happened on the rare occasion that an agent or manager pleaded and the actor was very special). As my reputation as a coach grew, more and more actors starting coming to me and I realized there was a huge lack of training when it came to auditioning. I also noticed that a lot of 'acting-teachers-slash-gurus' in LA were going to Atlanta and 'teaching' workshops. What this really meant is that quite often they were sending an underling to teach in their place, exploiting their name, fame, and their 'LA-Coach to-the-Stars' title.

The problem I was encountering in LA was that all of the actors who came to me from these studios to coach had spent years of their lives, thousands of dollars, and yet still had no idea how to prepare for an audition. At the risk of losing my tough, no bullshit reputation, it did break my heart. I wanted that to change, so I created a two-day audition intensive that could bring immediate results and help actors navigate the room and start booking. I was certain people would queue around the block for this lesson, so I came to Atlanta . and one person signed up. I gave away three other spots, and had a tremendous weekend with those four actors. They all immediately started booking. At the time, I knew that I really liked Atlanta. As a California native, I had never experienced anything like the southeast; I liked it, I liked the trees, the weather, and that people were nice. What I didn't know was the of the magnitude of jobs and opportunities for the working-class actor to the extent that I know now.

It had gotten to the point where in Los Angeles, my working actors weren't auditioning as much as they needed to be. An actor without an audition in sight is an actor without hope. Hopeless actors pose problems, which is why I require that all the actors in my class are actively auditioning. Let me say this about the Atlanta market: there is a huge amount of potential, but there is still work to be done.

That being said, I'm seeing a massive shift and the opportunities here are endless, to be perfectly honest. We have actors booking jobs every single day; of the twenty or thirty people who moved here because of me, I would say ninety-eight percent of them are auditioning at minimum quadruple the amount they were in Los Angeles. They also are able to have a life, since the cost of living is lower than Los Angeles or New York. More and more actors are booking recurring and series regulars out of Atlanta, and in the past year I've had eight actors flown to LA from Atlanta to test for (and subsequently book) pilots.

For so many people, the dream has always been LA, but as someone who has lived through the hell that can be that industry and considers herself a true survivor and innovator, Atlanta provides an environment that, while not without its issues and problems, is filled with hope and possibilities for actors. For the majority of actors, the bottom line is that this is a numbers game. To see actors auditioning one to ten times a week is extraordinary. My Los Angeles actors who are series regulars, are going to continue working and I will continue working with them. I still go out to LA between three and six times a year. It's a huge leap and I know that Hollywood is 'THE place to be', however, I think Atlanta is a wonderful option for working actors.

Both Marissa (The incredible person who runs the studio) and myself continuously find ourselves shaking our heads in amazement at not only the number of our actors who are working, but the kinds of roles they are getting to audition for. It is not just a co-star market anymore. My hope for the Southeast to cement our place in the film and television landscape by being known for having trained, reliable talent.

My suggestion is simple. Get here. Actors who are trying to straddle both worlds and have an agent before leaving (probably to make sure the move will work) are causing problems. There is a huge local hire tax credit, and when actors don't physically live here, it screws the actors, agents, and casting when you need to be on set within twenty-four hours but can't get on a flight. If you have your materials together, a great reel, a few credits, phenomenal training, or if you just know how to work hard and be a great CEO of your own company, you will do well in Atlanta. What traditionally takes actors ten or even twenty years in Los Angeles, in my experience can only take two to five years in Atlanta.

CONCLUSION

I have been brutally honest and direct throughout this book. However, now, i would like to talk to you. The actor, the artist, the soul who has chosen the path less traveled. The path of maximum resistance.

I want everyone reading this to know that I see miracles happen daily. Whether that is an actor with no credits getting flown out from Florida to test as the lead in a series in LA, or an actor who has been at it for five years – five long, disappointing, fruitless years – taking my intensive and booking their first co-star. I've taken actors who are in a dry spell to a windfall of work just by making a few suggestions and by urging them to take risks. To get back in the ring. Make no mistakes, that is where we live. In a boxing ring. A gladiator's arena. I know I've used a lot of analogies, but we are boxers. No's are punches; not getting the role, consistently turning in good work, auditioning for years with no results, well, it leaves scars. It leaves us bloodied and bruised, yet we have to look and act as if we've never been touched. This is a career of how many times you get up, not how many punches you've taken. I ask you this: if after years of work and rejection, you get the call saying you've booked it, is the journey worth it? If the answer is no, then please, I urge you, find a career that will love you back. For most of you, if you've gotten this far, I assume the answer would be yes. I applaud you. I am proud of you. Raise your bar. Work harder. Demand excellence.

And yes, get back into the ring. Never doubt that you are part of the future of acting. You are already ahead of the curve by virtue of taking an Intensive with me or by reading this book.

Hollywood is leading the charge, embracing change and tearing its existing structures down, but we still have a long way to go. The actor has been the lowest on the proverbial totem pole, little more than a joke, for way too long. I want to inform and empower my people. Actors need to get out of class and into reality. It takes decades to work and many still don't 'make it'. You have to be a warrior, a gladiator, a competitor. The artist cannot survive in the arena with today's methods of teaching. I am sick of actors getting taken advantage of, and I am tired of actors not understanding the reality of what it takes to work. We must as a community grow, always look to become smarter or wiser, because truthfully, we hold the power to have a massive impact on this world . . . We have the potential to write the future. Those are the actors and people I train.

Be brave. Be fearless and unrelenting in your pursuit of your dream. Surround yourself with love. Discover yourself and be honest with what you see and feel. If something hurts, let it hurt; cry and then get back up. Get used to being uncomfortable. Someone once told me the worst way an actor can feel is comfortable. Volunteer. Recognize how much you have to give. Make your world bigger, never smaller. Ask questions. Say thank you. Realize that as an actor, you can make people laugh. You can encourage them to feel. When someone tries to tell you all the reasons you shouldn't, keep telling yourself all the reasons you should. And that nothing, absolutely nothing is impossible in this career.

I hope this has helped you – given you words and advice you've been seeking, the class you've been looking so hard to find – and know this book is for you. Yours is the braver path to take in life, and I'm proud of you.

With Love, Coach

INTERVIEWEE CREDITS

JENNIFER COOPER, Casting Director
MacGyver, Hawaii Five-O, Magnum P.I., Cold Case, Whiskey Cavalier

ETHAN EMBRY, Actor
First Man, Grace and Frankie, Once Upon a Time, Sneaky Pete, The Walking Dead, Hawaii Five-O, Brotherhood

SHERRY THOMAS, Casting Director
Handmaid's Tale, Breaking Bad, Twilight Zone, Barry, The Walking Dead, Gotham, Better Call Saul

JESSE WILLIAMS, Actor
Grey's Anatomy, The Cabin in the Woods, The Butler, The Sisterhood of the Traveling Pants 2, Beyond the Break

CHRISTINA OCHOA, Actor
Animal Kingdom, Valor, A Million Little Things, Blood Drive, Matador

JASON LOCKHART, Agent
Head of Film and Television, Atlanta Talent and Models

INTERVIEWS

JENNIFER COOPER

Can you tell me how you became a casting director?

I went to Emerson College and moved here with the LA program they offered where you intern for a semester. I got an internship with Mali] Finn Casting. After two weeks of interning in the casting office, I quickly decided I did not want to be an actress. That interning job led me to an assistant job on *Cold Case* and then I just continued to work from there.

What is the most common mistake actors make regarding choices?

Making a choice to be different instead of making a choice that is justified in the scene is a mistake. For example, if you do a scene in a car and you decide to stand, that would not be justified. Making an obvious choice doesn't make you blend in, as long as you make the choice, in the way that you think.

How far is too far to go with a choice in the room? (Do you have any stories?)

A good casting director, I think, understands that what you see in the room is obviously not what you're going to get on set. So I think you make choices that better your audition and anything that is sort of extraneous to that I don't think you need to do. I don't think you need to bring a knife to show that you're scary. I don't think you need to kiss the casting director to prove that it's romantic. And I don't think you need to bring a bat in your pants to prove that you're a thug. All of these things have happened. Sometimes, an actor will ask me, for example, "There's a knock in the scene, do you mind if I knock when I start?" Well, I guess that's okay, but is that really going to move your character forward?

I think you want to make choices that you really identify as choices that could better your three-minute audition. I don't think any choice is too far off if what comes of it is brilliant. I don't think any choice is wrong if when a casting director or a writer or producer sees it and goes, "Oh my god, they're amazing and that choice fueled what they're doing." The times the choices become ridiculous is when it doesn't land and it doesn't make sense. Then, people start to wonder what you're doing and they start to ask, "Why did you do that?

When an actor is labeled 'green,' what does that mean to you?

I don't think 'green' necessarily has [anything] to do with talent; I think it has to do with experience. The audition experience is something that takes practice. It's not just about having raw talent. So I don't know that green refers to how talented you are so much as how experienced you are. Do you understand how the process works? Do you identify the cues in the room? Do you know how to read a room, the casting director, and the producers? Do you know how to work with the reader? I think it's a term that refers to understanding that there's much more that goes into booking a job than just raw talent. It's not an acting class. It's not a theater class in college. It's a really specific set of criteria. I really believe a lot of it comes in knowing the casting directors, the shows, and the tone of the network. Understanding comedy versus drama.

Understanding one hour versus half hour. It's not like I call someone in and they're bad and I call them green. Usually, green refers to someone who does have talent, and you say, "I see that there's something there, but they just don't understand the mechanism that runs this industry," as opposed to, "I'm just not seeing what this is." I rarely describe someone untalented as green. There are some people I see and think, "Okay, you're going to be on tape doing that?" There are some people who I see who I don't think understand the craft, or are in it for the right reasons, or have trained. I think there are a lot of those people.

I don't think, for me, there's much benefit in saying, "This person was bad and I never want to see him again." I tend to make criticisms of people who I think are good. I want to be constructive. I don't want to waste my time with people who I think are really, truly just on another planet. I could give a thirty-minute presentation on how inappropriate it is to give me your headshot in a public place or restaurant and after the presentation, have someone from the audience try to give me their headshot in the parking lot. There are some people who are just in it for the wrong reason and it doesn't matter what I say. So I try to just not give any feedback, constructive or not constructive to people who I don't think have any potential.

What does it mean to "read the room"?

In terms of reading the room with casting directors and producers, I think sometimes you go into a room and you say hi and they say hi and you just start. Sometimes we're stressed and just want to get to the read. I think a big mistake actors commonly make is letting that affect them too much. It has nothing to do with you. You don't know what happened in their day. I've seen producers who don't give a single nod or anything in the room and the actor walks out and he says, "He's great, we should give it to him." I've also noticed that sometimes, actors will go over the top and start to tell a story or tell a joke. What you're trying to do is stand out, but all they're going to remember is whether you were right or wrong for the role. You could be the nicest person and they could think it falls flat. Or you could be quiet before and they think you're great. To me, it shows [as] amateur when someone comes in and they're trying to work the room because if everyone did that, by the thirtieth time, the person who doesn't do that becomes appealing. It's enough to walk in and say, "Hi, how are you?"

What do you recommend regarding questions before the audition?

I think most casting directors ask if you have any questions. If you don't, don't ask a question. A common mistake I see is the actor makes up a question because she thinks she's supposed to or the actor summarizes what she's about to do. And that happens all the time. For example, "I was just thinking this person is sort of dark…" And when she finished the summary, I say, "Okay, let's see that." And that's tough because if you've just explained what you're going to do, you better do it and you better be very good. I think five out of ten actors who walk into my room summarize. It doesn't matter if the actor asks me a question or not in the room, it's about the read. That's it. Ask a question if you have one. For example, ask if you don't know how to pronounce something and it's tripping you up. Ask [about] a character in the scene who you can't find out who that person is and you've already tried research. Ask if it's something that will help you own that audition better. If someone is coming in for a one-line co-star and they ask about their back-story, I wonder how that will inform their audition. But if someone has a ten-page audition and they think one line references the fact that they were abused as a child, that would be a good question to ask because that can change the whole audition. I think you have to ask yourself if you're honestly asking because the question will affect your audition. If not, don't ask it.

What is something you think actors misunderstand about the auditioning process?

Actors are selling a product, themselves. This means they are responsible for their mental care. When someone is worried about his SAG insurance or somebody broke up with her boyfriend the night before or someone has family problems, it shows. If you're not keeping yourself in mental check, it shows in the room. Whether or not you think it shows, it does. It's an intuition thing. When someone's off his game, you know it.

How should actors respond to feedback from casting directors?

Part of this is learning the casting director. Some casting directors, if they love you, won't give you a single direction. It has to be you, delivering consistently good work. If you're in the place where you're doing good work, then you're probably able to self-evaluate your situation.

What should an actor do after the audition?

Leave and let it go because no matter what you put into it after you leave, it has zero effect on the outcome. So, it can't be healthy It would only be worth it if you could affect the outcome. So play a hobby or volunteer because whatever you carry with you bleeds over into the next audition.

You have to be looking forward, not backward. Learn the mistakes you made and change for the next one, but then move on.

What should you change from the pre-read to the callback?

If you do a pre-read and you get a callback, whatever you did worked. If you get a note, then go with that note. I think you do whatever was the last thing that worked in the room. I think it's a huge mistake to drastically change what you did from the initial read to the callback. I think it's a common mistake for someone to get the callback and then work on it too much in the direction, with a coach who gives them a totally new way to go. If it worked, it worked and you should stick with that.

What are some of the smartest choices you've seen actors make in a room?

Something I think is important and very few people do is not just research on the role, but also research on the genre and the tone. Your audition is so informed by what network it's for, what type of show it is, and understanding what's been happening in the show. It blows me away when someone walks in for an audition and they've never seen an episode of the show. I'm not saying go watch six seasons of the show; watch ten minutes of the show. Know the differences between the networks. ABC is family oriented. FOX is like 24; shoot 'em up.

CBS is procedural. There's so much that you can learn having nothing to do with your audition, that you can learn before you go in. With pilot season, it's so difficult because all you have is the network. Actors make their lives so much more difficult by not controlling the things they can control, like have great headshots. Does someone who works at *Goldman Sachs* not have a perfectly prepared resume? Your whole life is based on your headshot for a really long time. You can go to class and train. You can control that. You can coach on auditions that you're not fully grasping. You can research the tone of the show and the network. So for me, the really good choices are the really obvious ones. Everyone says, "How could you be an actor?

There are so many?" The truth is that there are not that many actors who are really prepared. You are not in a huge pool of people who understand that basic necessities of being an actor. It's your job to be healthy. It's your job to train. If I hear another actor say acting class and coaching is too expensive. Literally, when I moved out here as an actor, I got six of my friends together from theater school and we practiced scenes in a basement for free. You can do it. "I don't do plays because LA theater is bad." Well, then do some good LA theater. The list of excuses is never ending for why you're not working. My favorite excuse of all time is my agent and manager are bad. "Really? Why do you think that might be?" If you're controlling the other things, you'll get an amazing agent and manager.

This whole business is a catch 22. "I can't get into SAG because I can't get a job. I can't get a job because I can't get SAG." But somehow people did it. So, you could choose to rise above them and make your own way. In this age, we have free distribution. *YouTube* is unbelievable. You have free distribution. It took people not in our generation creating full-blown movies if they wanted to get anything scene. "I don't have a demo tape, so I can't get a job." Go and make a short scene with a friend that's fabulous and use that as your demo tape. Everyone has these excuses. And I'm not saying they're not valid. It is an uphill climb. But all of those things are standing in your way all the time. You have to assume that the person next to you is doing more than you, so you can only do more and more and train harder and harder. You have to do more if you want to compete in this business.

What's something you think might surprise people about your job?

Casting directors are on your team. So many people think that the casting director is the enemy. You have to just think, if nothing else, if I'm the worst casting director in the world and I hate actors and I want nothing to do with them, my day depends on casting an actor. I don't go home unless they're cast. So, there's nothing I want more in the world than to cast an actor so I did my job. It's not like I'm ever watching an actor and thinking to myself, "Oh, I hope this person fails." My hope for every actor who comes in is for him to be the actor who gets the job. And I don't think that onus falls as much on a producer, writer, or director.

What would you think if an actor followed up with you after, perhaps in the form of a thank you note? And how do you feel about postcards?

When I explain to someone the amount of work I do in a day and the amount of time I have, I ask them if they think I'm going to sit down and look through postcards and be like, "Oh my god, this actor is on *Medium* next Tuesday." I just don't have the time. I think acting is already very expensive and time consuming and I think the time could be so much better spent doing the things that I think really do affect change in your career. With that being said, I have heard some other casting directors read every postcard. I don't. I can only be specific that I never look at a postcard. I do care that people are booking work. I do watch a lot of television to try to see that. But more importantly, I read the actor's resume. Regarding a card or a gift, I think you send one when you book a job. I don't think you send one when you get an audition. In general, I think a card is very kind and plenty and you don't need to send a gift. But if you pre-read with a casting director and you book a series regular, sure, send him a bottle of wine. But I don't think it's the actor's responsibility by any means to engage in feeling grateful that a casting director gave you an audition. You earned it. To me, it's a sign of [an] amateur. I've gotten two postcards delivered to my house with actors' faces on them. That's inappropriate. So often, you hear, "I know I shouldn't do this, but..." or "I know I shouldn't say this, but..." "I don't normally do this, but..." If any of those things are about to come out of your mouth, the answer is, don't do it. Don't do it. When you go on a date and the guy calls you thirty times the next day, that's wrong. I think that really common knowledge applies to this. It's not brain surgery. Do you bring a picture with your face and to date with the reasons you're a successful businessperson? No. You're just good at your job.

If there isn't a camera in the room, what, if anything, should actors do differently?

Nothing. Do absolutely nothing different unless you're auditioning in a theater where you feel like you need to project to be heard. A room is small. I can hear you. You don't need to audition directly to the camera. You have a right when you're being filmed to move a little. Having no camera doesn't mean you should be running and walking all through the scene. What I'm looking for is the nuances of your eyes and facial expressions and your tone and the story you're telling. That shouldn't change whether I'm filming it or not. The majority of pre-reads that are filmed are never seen because if they liked you, the casting director will bring you back, unless it's being booked off tape. The camera means very little. You're never going to have huge, big movements. You have to act within your medium. It's a tiny medium and it should be treated that way. You should never be doing things big because you're afraid they're going to be missed. If you act big, it reads big and that translates to, "They're really theater-y."

How much and in what forms do you electronically research actors you are considering? (Ex: Facebook, Google, IMDb)

I look at your *IMDb* and I look at your reel. So I need to see wherever that's available. So if you have a website that has your reel on it, I need that. If you have a *Vimeo* account or *Breakdown Express* that has your reel, that's all I need.

What do you suggest if there's a gun or a sex scene?

I think you have to do what benefits your audition. Coming from CSI, I tend to notice that when someone's fake holding a fake gun, they're empowered by it. I don't think you need to bring a prop gun. As for a sex scene, don't strip in front of a producer. Don't make the people in the room uncomfortable. Judge the scene in the room and do what you need to do to be great.

What are your thoughts about being off book?

You should be familiar with the material. Glancing down is totally cool.

What makes a great headshot?

You want to look like your picture and you don't want your picture to be so specific that it is a character type. It should be your essence of who you are as opposed to geared toward a specific character.

What can you generally advise to actors when they're just getting to LA?

Get into an acting class because it's the best way to create a community with actors. They're your best allies. They'll tell you the dos and don'ts. You're not going to get it any straighter than anyone who's been working for ten years.

What is a pet peeve that actors do that drives you crazy?

When there isn't common courtesy, it bugs me. When people are being snippy with other actors or with assistants that bothers me. We're all busy. We're all tired. We all got stuck on the 405. You have to approach the people you work with out of respect, everyone from the PA to the producer. Because if I work really hard to respect every actor from the one-line co-star to the series regular, it bothers me when that kind of respect isn't returned.

Does what I wear actually affect if I get the role or not?

Sure. I think if you come in for a lawyer and you wear a punk rock outfit, it's hard to get past. I don't think it's 'make it or break it,' but I think the idea is to wear something that hints at the character. You don't come in costume. For example, don't come in wearing a nurse's outfit.

What do I do if I mess up on a line?

If it totally threw your audition and you're not going to be able to recover, I think you say, "I'm really sorry, would it be alright if I start over?" If it didn't throw you, then keep going. No one is going to think you're a bad actor because you messed up on one of the lines.

When there's more than one person in the scene, to whom should I deliver the lines?

All the lines should be directed at the reader so that you have a connection. I don't think you have to play it to a fake person to the left of the reader. If it massively helps you, it's okay, but I think it's better to play everything to the reader.

Should I pantomime anything (typing, texting, etc.)?

If it helps you, yes.

What can I do as an actor to positively differentiate myself from other actors in my demographic?

The answer is please don't try to differentiate yourself. You are unique because you're unique as a human being. Nothing that you do is what sets you apart from another person. If thirty people read the exact same thing and do the exact same choices, it's thirty different takes. You cannot be the exact same as someone else. It's impossible.

Should an actor wear the same thing to a callback?

Wear either the same thing or something similar.

What is the most important thing to do in the audition?

I think the most important thing is to understand the essence of the role.

Does an actor need to go into the room and feel as if he needs to switch?

No, not at all. If anything, after the scene, the actor could say, "Oh god, sorry, I got prepped and I came in. Thanks for having me." You could show the switch after if you really needed to do prep work before if you really feel like you want to differentiate yourself from the scene. No one is going to fault you for doing an emotional scene. Everyone understands it's hard to come in and do an emotional scene. And if you do great work, they don't care that you came in crying. They care what it looks like the second that they say action. How you got there isn't their concern. I also think we should add with that that prep work is done outside of the audition. You would think that's an obvious thing, but many actors come in and say, "Can I have a minute?" and take a really long time usually of doing whatever they need to do. Most of those people fall flat because if you are putting that kind of pressure on yourself to prove that you're doing good work, you better be pretty serious when you start. Everyone after seeing you prep is expecting to see something pretty serious when you start. It sets you up to fail. If you need to do that because you're about to blow them away, then do it. Anything short of that, do it outside of the room. When something is really emotional and the actor comes in already in that place, the casting director, assuming he's good at his job, will not be super excited and will not respond to the actor with a lot of mismatched energy. The casting director is supposed to be in tune with the actor

What are some common mistakes you see actors making on their resume?

Lying. I don't think you should lie on your resume. I also don't think when you don't have a lot of credits it benefits you to put a bunch of random stuff like theater in high school. I'd rather you had a shorter resume that was actually full of pertinent information for me than filling a huge resume with nothing I've ever heard of.

Does it matter if you come in as union or not?

In order for me to hire a non-union actor, I have to prove that there was not a qualified union actor that I could find. If, for example, there is a special skill that is required, then I could Taft-Hartley that person. It's hard to say that there is no one in the union who could fill that position. How should an actor prepare for a basic meeting with a casting director?

I think the actor should do some basic research of the casting director and what she does, the network she works on and the shows. Have some general information and just be prepared to be open and talk about yourself and what you want. Ask questions about what they're looking for. A general meeting is really an open conversation.

I think you have to think of it like any job interview. If you go in and you're super arrogant and you seem hard to work with, people don't want to work with you. If you seem really insecure and scared, they're worried that you're going to be insecure and scared on set. Whatever you're projecting in the room is what they assume you'll be like on set. This is something they're thinking about because it's not just, "Oh, I've hired them and it's over." It's, "Oh, I've hired them and now I have to see what I can get out of them on set."

ETHAN EMBRY

What is part of your daily routine that you feel is crucial to your growth as an actor?

People watching is one of those things that helps as far as things that apply to actors and the craft. Also, engaging. Just simple things, like at the grocery store or the gas station. Strike up small conversations. Talking and getting more outside of yourself is important. The more outside of ourselves we can be, the better. The more you pick up on body language and where they're at. The more you know about people, the better the portrayal. You start noticing human reaction. The more we experience, the more we can emulate. I probably could do more of that. Also, I meditate everyday.

From all of your experience, what is one piece of advice for a newer actor?

There was one thing that Ed O'Neill taught me when I was a kid. He pulled me into his trailer when I was 10, during lunch. He told me I should always try to remember this. Your job is no more important than anyone else's on this set. It's a collaborative effort and just because you have a trailer and you're getting paid more, and they're going to treat you differently, doesn't mean you are. Working in film is a very collaborative, union environment. It's union based. It's teamsters, electricians, grips, painters, a lot of workingmen and women. It's thought to be glamorous environment and it can be if you want it to be. But it's not going to benefit you. It's going to end up sheltering you from a lot of things. The more down to earth, real, and grounded that we can keep ourselves throughout the success and the struggle, the better off we'll all be. We get glamorized a little bit as actors in success and we have to take it. It's really just a marketing tool. Don't buy into the marketing tool.

I just become a part of it. I go up to people on set and introduce myself and say thank you. The project I'm working on now, for example, there are people on set who, if they're making anything, they're not making much. Be easy to work with. Show your appreciation because they're there working hard to make you and the whole project look better. If the project succeeds, we as actors get the accolades, so showing your appreciation is key. If you treat them like they're on your level, the environment on set is so much better. It's set up to separate some people. To lose the separation makes things so much better. It makes people want to be there. You can tell a difference when people aren't nervous and on edge. For example, the other day, there was an actor working and it was obvious he wanted to set a certain vibe. When he was done and left, everyone went back to having fun and wanting to be there and things ran more smoothly.

Before you were going out on a lot of auditions, how did you spend your time?

One of the biggest things that is most important for actors is that you have to have something else. If this is all you have to occupy your time, you will go crazy. It's not that you need to have a backup plan, but you need something else. I suggest having another art form because you're not going to be able to express yourself artistically as much as you would like to. You have to wait for people to give you the ability to perform as an artist. It's not like you can just go around acting all day. A musician can pick up his guitar anytime he wants to. He doesn't have to wait for someone to allow him to do it. Taking four different classes is awesome, but we don't necessarily always have that luxury because classes are expensive. I play the guitar and I spend time with my son. Having a fulfilling outside life is key. If we don't have a full life outside of our craft, then we're not going to emulate life very well. The more full our lives outside of our craft, the more full our lives can be. I spend my time trying to make my life as big as possible.

How did you get your start?

It's funny because I try to think about that and I don't really know. I remember growing up in a trailer park, then I started working and suddenly, we're living in a nice house and somewhere along the way, I fell in love with it. It's one of those beautiful accidents. It's all I know. The film business in my business. And I don't know how it started. I think not going to school and having social interaction; the film set was my first social experience. I fell in love with sets because of having that social interaction. I equate peers with set. I got lucky enough to keep getting booked.

Are you afraid of being typecast?

No, because if you do that, that means you played that guy really well. I would be more afraid of not being able to shake it off when I got home. I've played darker characters that I've not been able to shake for a long time. Leave your work at work. Not so much being typecast. That's doing your job; that's success. I like a challenge. Typecast me. I'll prove you wrong.

What odd jobs have you taken on to support yourself while pursuing acting?

I've been so blessed; I've never made a dollar doing anything but acting. That's not to say that I wouldn't because I'm down for that challenge too. I was listening to Sam Rockwell talk once and he was at the point of delivering burritos because he was turning down roles that he didn't believe in. While he was a known actor, he was delivering burritos to pay the bills. He believed that acting was an art form. He said he found that he was happier delivering burritos than being on a television show that he didn't believe in.

What makes a great meeting with potential representation?

It depends on where you are with your career. I don't ever look at whom they're representing. After I've made the decision that I like the person, I look then to make sure there's no conflict of interest. To me, it all boils down to who's willing to put in the work. It's about who'll dig in their heels and know that they might be working for free for a while, but they have to be willing to put in the investment. There has to be faith and support, of course. It's tough because that's a really personal thing. People have to find what they want in the representation for themselves. I kind of like a down to earth family guy; other people are going to want their person to be out and about. Your representation is, I think, a very personal thing. As long as you're comfortable, that's the key. If you can find someone who believes in you who works at ICM, then jump on it. But if you have to go to a smaller agent, one who is willing to work for you, then who cares what it says on the letterhead. You need someone who is willing to hit the pavement for you and pick up the phone.

Do you suggest people attend networking events (charities, etc.)?

I think that being charitable with your time is so important, especially as an actor, to gain perspective. The events are pretty gangster too. There's one charity I work with, and the night before the Golden Globes, it's the biggest turn out. The bigger you make your life, the more you experience, the better of an actor you'll become. You have to be open to new situations and new emotions. The more open you are, the better actor you'll be.

How do you prepare for an audition, beginning with getting the sides/ script to the actual first audition?

Lately, I've been finding myself in the character instead of trying to create the character they're looking for. I think words are important, of course, but finding a way for them to work for you, just getting comfortable with yourself, that's important. I think it's key to run it with another person before you go in there. Try as hard as you can to turn the audition experience that has so many negative connotations like feeling judged and picked apart into how lucky you are to have that opportunity to go in and audition. Find the good stuff. Know that there are twenty people who would kill to have that opportunity. Once you realize you're really blessed to have that audition, you're going to cherish that audition and your performance will improve. And then don't worry. It's tough, because when it's your bread and butter, to free yourself up so that you can really listen [is difficult.] When you're in your head in an audition, you probably do less than you do in any other instance. If you're not listening, you can't do the job. Just treat it like work and try not to take it personally. If you don't get the part, it's got nothing to do with that. There are a million variables that go into their decision. Who knows what they're looking for? I try to get out of my head, but sometimes, I don't succeed. If I don't like it, and I know I can do better and I've found a way to get out of my head, then I say, "That sucked, let me start over." It's just understanding that auditions can sometimes just be a crap-chute. It's about just going in there and being open and being available and just riding it out. It's tough. You'll see the one person who books and books, so you want to ask him what his secret is, but I don't think that there really is a secret.

What's some of the good advice you've gotten from casting directors or coaches?

Stay open. Be available when you walk into the room. Those are the things that I've found that when I apply them, they work. This town is full of different advices, and you have to find what works for you on a more consistent basis. Sometimes, that one thing that works for you won't work on a consistent basis. I remember Sara told me that I needed to fall in love with doing it again. Because it had become a place of stress and work, and it had so many other things attached to it. That changed a lot of other things for me. I fell in love with it again by working with other actors and watching their progress. Sara put me in a position where I could be of service, which made me realize what I do know about it. She coached me by letting me coach. I had gotten to a place where I thought I was a con artist. I thought I was getting paid a lot of money for something that wasn't deserved. Then, I realized what I do have, and that I have been slowly acquiring information over twenty-five years, which made me fall in love with it again. Smart coach.

I had never verbalized what I would go through before; I just did it. My whole process was internal, so I didn't realize how much went into it until I taught it. Like tapping into those parts of me that maybe weren't my daily personality, but there's a little bit of everyone in all of us. There's a small part of every character in everyone, even if it's something that we push away. Having that ability, even when you're playing characters who are not of the highest social standing. One of the hardest parts of my field is to be completely honest with yourself, but as actors, we have to be, because otherwise our actions are full of shit. For me, it's really personal, which is dangerous sometimes. Most of those things, you're not going to want to share with other people. It's looking at things from a clear perspective. If I'm angry, I'll smile first, but it's important to be more honest. If I don't like a person, I won't excuse myself. And it's tough. I'm no fucking saint, but I'm trying. And you don't have to be completely honest with everyone; not even with every friend, but you do need to be honest with some people. You can probably [see] who needs to hear that you're doing great and who needs to hear that you're doing shitty.

By looking at someone, you can see what he or she needs. To be able to look at someone and say, "I'm not doing so good" is important. "I'll be fine, but I'm not doing so great right now." If you aren't in touch with your own emotions, you can't truly find a character. You have to be completely honest with your own thoughts, emotions, and actions to be able to apply those thoughts, emotions, and actions to another character. If you're playing a broad character, then you might get deeper with it, but the start is, "How would I react to this?"

How do you deal specifically with intimate scenes? Do you spend a lot of time getting to know the other actor?

The last movie I did was my first sex scene, and it was not at all like a sex scene, it was a comedy. It's interesting. I'll play husbands and boyfriends and have kissing scenes, but it's a dangerous line, especially if you're in a relationship because you have to identify with the person and it's like when you're playing someone's boyfriend, you're going to hang out with them and you're supposed to be looking for the good things. The situation hasn't presented itself a lot in my adult life. Not a happily married role. As you get older, the roles get more realistic and you start playing unhappily married people, which is easy. That's a personal thing; people are going to deal with it differently. You just have to find what works for you and be willing to change it immediately if you feel it's not working. If you found a way that works for you, but it's completely opposite and damaging for the other person, you better not use that. You better be open to change. You better be willing to flip shit on a dime, all the time.

How do you reinvigorate yourself and your career when you've been in a booking slump?

Again, it depends on where you're at in your career. For me, I have to realize that I'll be okay. I have to realize I've been doing this my whole life and I'll book again. I tried to cash out on my pension a few months ago and the next day I booked a job. Plus, they wouldn't let me cash out my pension until I'm 55 years old. You may feel like you'll never book again, that's a lie you tell yourself.

JASON LOCKHART

There's the idea that agents in Atlanta will sign anyone. How true is that?

Not true at all. I don't even want to consider someone unless every single local casting director has already booked them. I want to make money off of them tomorrow, not six months from now after they've gotten accustomed to the way the market works, who's here, and how Atlanta operates.

In LA I tell my actors that once you have a great agent you are going to need two to three years to really start booking. Here, you're saying that you aren't interested in them if you can't make money off of them within six months?

Not even that. If I can't make money off of them tomorrow, then it doesn't make sense for me. I have a roster that is way too full – hundreds and hundreds of people – so for me, they need to be immediately marketable.

What made you make the switch from Los Angeles to Atlanta?

I was intrigued. I was very much living in stasis in Los Angeles. Making a certain amount of money, doing a certain thing, always promised more but never really having that promise be delivered. Running the race. Tasting small successes, but still always hungry and never satisfied, chasing all kinds of dreams that sidetrack you from what is realistic. I felt like most of my day was either self-indulgent or unfulfilling. The opportunity came, and I was ready for the move. I had been in LA for way too long, since 2008, and it just wasn't realistic. I wasn't going to buy a house in Beverly Hills, I didn't want to move way out into the Valley and have to drive two hours into work every day while working seventy plus hours a work every week.

Has LA become almost unmanageable?

There's just too many people and not enough space. Too many people and not enough jobs. Too many people on the road, not enough lanes.

What's the difference between the Atlanta and Los Angeles markets?

If we parallel everything, then it becomes not just about the market but about the city. Here there is a lot of competition as well, there are a lot of people. But it is not as bad in terms of space, lanes, and opportunities.

You mentioned you felt like you were running a race in LA. Do you feel like that has changed since you've been in Atlanta?

Oh yeah. I love it here. Because I feel like I run just as hard and just as fast, and although I love a lot of the agents here in town, I feel like my training and the coaches I had, and my drive when I wake up every day is faster than many.

There are some people here who run really hard and really fast, and I love them because it feels like we are alongside each other, going through the same things, almost like I can high-five them while we are running, but there are a lot of people here who I'm running much faster than. And it's great because in LA you can run really hard and really fast, but then you smash into a wall. Here, you can run really hard and really fast and break through that wall every single day. And when I break through that wall, I'm taking people with me. I'm not really doing it for myself. It's my job. But I'm taking people with me who could never get through unless someone ran really hard and really fast for them. And I get to show them the other side of the wall. I did it three times this morning before 9:00 AM.

Meaning?

Bookings. Exciting bookings. Helping them achieve their dreams. Not just their dreams of being a working actor, but putting food on the table, or paying off their student debt, or supporting their family by making money as an actor. Some people in Los Angeles literally never make a dollar, but here I've got a lot of people making a year's salary that is much better than other jobs and getting full health insurance and benefits for themselves and for their family.

What is it that most takes away from your time or ability to run through these walls for your actors?

That's a great question. I actually just answered this on a panel the other night. I probably get over a thousand emails a day, and of those thousand, at least eight hundred of them are emails I don't need to receive. They don't put money in my pocket, or my clients' pockets, or do anything other than feed some sort of ego or unrealistic hope. Probably eighty percent of the emails I receive have absolutely nothing to do with realistic dollars

And how many of those are from actors?

Eighty to ninety percent. Things like, "Am I still on avail?", "Have you submitted me for anything?", "Have you heard about this job?", "Did you see my audition?" None of that matters. Doesn't matter if I like it. Every now and then I'll see an audition and hate it, so I'll tell them to do it again, but what if they don't book it because I tell them I hated it? It's just an opinion and it is so subjective.

There's a rumor here that the fast you get an audition in, the more likely you are to book. Is this true?

I think that happens sometimes. But I can think of two times out of maybe twelve thousand times that something like that happened. It isn't something I would put all my time and energy into because those numbers are so small, but yes, it is possible. It depends on the office. Some casting directors will do that, some won't, and some do it simply because the producers are demanding they send the tapes as they come.

We are hearing some of the things that actors should not be asking. Do you have any more?

Almost anything an actor needs to ask their agent can be found online. Especially with SAG questions. I've had to explain SAG payment scales so many times, and that isn't part of my job description. That's taking time out of my day where I could be helping other actors or even the person asking the question get auditions, but instead I'm spending my time on the phone with you. Honestly, the actors that I never speak to are really the busiest. I know that sounds ridiculous because everyone thinks there is going to be this fifty-fifty partnership between themselves and their agent, but the actors that are making the most money are the ones who get emails – all of the information is in the email – they turn in their audition and forget about it, and then I tell them they booked and production will be in touch. I never really speak to them and they're making so much money. It's because their time is too valuable. I'm never on the phone with big producers. Why? Because they are way too busy. If I do speak to a big producer, or even the way that I speak to casting, our emails and text messages are a sentence long. They are brief. Because we are busy handling things realistically. Anytime I get an email that is long or has a lot of questions, it shows they want something from me, they have all the time in the world, and they aren't focused on something precise.

What are some of the things that you look for in a client here in Atlanta?

I love clients who trust me. They don't worry if they're right for this audition or not, or that they haven't heard from me in a week, or that they just got four auditions in a week and they think they're wrong for all of them.

Do people say that?

I feel like actors all the time look for a reason not to do an audition. Things like, "I just auditioned for this other role on Tuesday, and the shoot window is the same as this audition, so I shouldn't do this too". Like, no. I missed the part where you were avail checked, or booked. It happens all the time. Or the breakdown says 'scrawny' and they say, "I'm not scrawny" or "I never play the bad guy". It's ridiculous.

What do you think makes a great headshot?

I want to make sure that an actor's headshots represent them and the type that they really are, because we need to be sure that we are on the same page with that. Actors should not be sending me a file of hundreds of headshot options. Filter it down to four or five options for each look, and then I'll tell you what I think. But if you just choose the headshots that you think make you look the best, irrespective of how good they are for me, for what I'm doing, then I get frustrated because you are wasting my time. You should have pictures that aren't all glamorous. Have one in a V-neck with no makeup, because I can use that for a nurse, or an alcoholic mother, or a ton of stuff. It doesn't have to be too on-the-nose. Especially if you don't have a ton of credits and the casting directors don't know you. You should have photos that show you as your most marketable, not just you most attractive.

I talk about the importance of the thought behind the headshot. Have you noticed this in your work?

Yes! I represent a gorgeous actress here, but all of her headshots look like a glamorous actress. They look like a glossy version of who you are, not a real person that I can submit. I need to be able to submit a her as nurse, a blue-collar mom, or a white-collar lawyer. It doesn't have to be just in the wardrobe, but it needs to be in the thought as well. In the eyes. When shooting headshots, you need to be prepared like you would for an acting job. If you're a six foot, two-hundred-and-thirty-pound, muscular man, come prepared as a bouncer. Be living in that space and be ready to have a thought like, "you aren't getting in". Headshots are an acting job, not a photoshoot. Once you look at enough headshots, you can start to tell how good an actor is just based of their headshots.

What can a client do to make your job easier?

I asked an actor if they could ride horses for a breakdown, and less than two minutes later, he emailed me with a ton of proof and photos of what he could do. It was unbelievable quick, and I was able to send it to casting immediately. And we didn't even book that job, but then six months later, I saw another breakdown like that and forwarded his materials immediately. Less than five minutes later he had booked it, because I guarantee you no other agent or actor had been able to send that casting director a detailed pitch about what they could do so quickly. Sometimes it does pay to be the absolute first person in the door, so to speak.

Should actors send you everything they do?

No. That isn't my job. I don't need to see your short, or your play, or your stand-up comedy. A lot of the time when I do, I think, "Wow, they aren't as good as I thought. Why am I representing them?" If you're getting auditions, leave me alone and let me do my job. If there is a money issue, let's talk about it. But anything that feeds ego, not business, is not worth it. Also, learn to be concise, because that makes me want to work with you more. One sentence or less. Half the time, I won't even start with "hello". Sometimes that bothers people, but again my job is to get you paid, not ask how your personal life is. I'm too busy working for you and everyone else.

Should actors be looking for LA representation if they live in Atlanta?

I'm never looking for LA representation for my clients here. It does us no good. We live and work in Atlanta, and it makes no sense for us. We don't want to deal with another market that operates differently. The obvious exception is if a client makes a ton of money. Then it is worth it. We also won't represent people who are based in Los Angeles, and that makes casting directors love us. Again, unless you are a legitimate A-lister, it doesn't work. Casting directors want people who are local and available. We are Atlanta Models and Talent, and most of our actors work and live within a fifty-mile radius of Atlanta. It means that casting knows that if a date changes, or there's a last-minute fitting, or any kind of emergency, our people are actually here and will be ready. Plus, I've seen so many actors get a couple of credits here, move out to LA, and then completely bottom out. Going from two to three auditions a week to one audition a month is hard. And I've seen a ton of actors who have been struggling in LA for years come to Atlanta and book immediately. This market has a ton of opportunity

Do you think actors are making a mistake when they are trying to get agents in markets where they physically don't live?

I think it's indicative that whatever they are doing in that market isn't working, so they are trying to expand. Instead of expanding, they need to just leave and go to the new market. They need to take risks. That is what I did. I didn't try to be an agent in both LA and Atlanta. I wasn't trying to just get new clients or more money while not taking the risk. I made the move.

How can an actor be proactive when they aren't auditioning?

I think it's important to create content. I come from a background where I did a lot of things, wore a lot of hats in this industry. It has definitely helped me. Having the verbiage, knowing what everyone does, and understanding the industry is so important. Actors don't have a ton of power, and this helps you gain knowledge of the industry as a whole, which in turn gives you more power. Plus, it means you will be working. I know a huge writer who insists that a writer should always be writing at least one project, if not several simultaneously. Acting in any way, whether it's just doing scene, doing theatre, writing content, filming shorts, anything, will only help you.

Are the days of only being an actor over?

I think so. There needs to be a work ethic. Some of the best content comes from an actor with a desire to tell a story. Or play a strong objective. Go through an arc. They need to get it down on paper and try to make it happen.

Should actors still be self-submitting after they've signed with an agency?

For commercial, no. Because a lot of those contracts are trying to fuck actors over. Doing a soda commercial for a few hundred dollars in perpetuity so you can never do another soda commercial is a bad idea. For smaller projects and shorts, I think they should be. Be working. Be acting all the time, because it won't get in the way. If you book something big, I do ask that you say that your agent booked something way bigger and say that you won't be available that day. Maybe it will be a nightmare, but then you learn as well. I think it helps you learn what sets are good and what sets are bad.

Should an actor ever send you their materials unsolicited?

I mean I just hit delete all day long. I feel terrible, because they send these long emails with all their hopes and dreams, but I get such a high volume that I just have to delete them as fast as I can. I want my inbox to be empty so that I can attack important things in real time. I literally just delete all day long if it isn't something I don't have to respond to. A referral is really the only way it could even get noticed.

What can actors do to educate themselves?

Read. Read your whole sag contract. Do union events, and read the website. I've got books on my shelf. Get the book and read it. How hard is that? If you're working, you can ask the other actors on set questions. I don't mind helping if I have the time, but I almost never have time. And if the time that I do have needs to be spent on important things like negotiating actors a higher rate or improving the business. I have sixteen emails that came in since we've been talking, and how many of them are actually important? Probably none.

As you are building a career, how much creativity or freedom does an actor have? if you are going in for one line. You can do so much with one line. I love that you said not when you make it about you. Part of the reason I became an agent is that I no longer am living a self-indulgent life. My whole life is selfless, and I am getting so many rewards from the universe. Everything I do is trying to help other people. And it feels good. Which is why I stopped acting. It wasn't fulfilling, and it was always about me, and all my time, energy and focus was spent on me. It just didn't work for me. But the most successful actors are selfless as well. Their entire audition is about serving the story or their partner. And when an actor makes it about them, you can see it. You can see them worrying about how they look. Fuck all that. But when it is just about the story, especially when it is just one line, it works. The worst is when someone is attractive. They've been told they should be a movie star. The worst is when people are auditioning for shows like *The Resident* and they come in with full makeup. You're supposed to be a tired nurse who is falling asleep on the job, why are you in full makeup? You aren't auditioning to be Julia Robert's sister in a movie. Strip all that away. You are just a small part of the whole, just like a second AD. They just need to fill every position and they don't even always want to hire who's best; they want to hire who is not going to be an issue. That's why once you've been approved by a network, it is easier for you to get re-approved by that network again . They just don't want to hire someone who will show up late, or not do their lines, or talk too much on set.

There's an art form to becoming a recurring costar or guest star. Oh absolutely. Show up, sit in the corner, read a book, and when they call you go do your thing in one take. Go back to reading in the corner. Those directors and producers will love you. It isn't about becoming friends with everyone on set. And if you do need to be friends with the stars of the show, it is about learning how to be friends with them on their terms.

JESSE WILLIAMS

Before you were going out on a lot of auditions, how did you spend your time?

Once I decided I wanted to act, I spent my time in New York hustling. I was scouring papers and the Internet. I went to every SAG event that I could possibly find. I went to every workshop. I met every casting director I could. I went to networking events. I found ways to hustle the passwords of *Breakdown Services* to get breakdowns. I was in acting classes. I was seeing plays. I was doing readings with friends. I was offering to help my friends read for auditions or if they got work. I was working on student films, but not as an actor necessarily. I was shooting them working as a cinematographer or a grip or anything just to be on set. I was learning monologues. I'm also a very competitive person, so I was also playing sports. I was never wholly obsessed with acting. I did not eat, live, and breathe acting. I tried to keep a balance with family or friends. I tried to still have a social life.

What is part of your daily routine that you feel is crucial to your growth as an actor?

Unless I have to be on set at five or six, I try to go for a short twenty or thirty minute run to assess what my goals are for the day, clear my head, and get my blood pumping. For my lines, I always write my lines down. Even if it's two lines, I write it down in my own handwriting.

What took you from auditioning to booking?

The change occurred once I stopped being excited to just audition. At first, you're happy just to audition and the audition was the achievement. And of course, that will feel like an accomplishment. But once I started setting my sights past that, and I only auditioned for things that I fully expected to book, I had a change in mindset. I started auditioning, fully expecting to book the roles. It's like how in boxing you want to imagine punching through the other person, not punching them. I wanted to act for the job, not for the audition. Of course, it's 85% luck. If I could go back to the beginning of my career, I probably would've had this vision the whole time. I started acting later in life. I had a different job for years and years. So, I had a little bit of my own timeline pressure, more than a teenager, figuring out what to do in the industry. I had my own adult, New York pressures. I think auditioning is terrifying and bizarre. I just don't think there's that much time to waste. I would try to look beyond the audition.

How did you get a manager?

A manager was the last thing I got. I got a New York agency first, then a publicist, then a manager. I got a manager via my publicist and agent. I was of the thought process that you don't get a manager unless you have a career in motion to manage, or if you have so much going on that it's necessary. I'm not saying I believe that. That's just the school of thought I came from. For some people, they might not be the most important. There are so many different types of managers. For a long time, my publicist was my right-hand man.

What makes a great meeting with potential representation?

I think that depends, because I've done meetings with zero career momentum and then meetings with the momentum that I've had recently. Everything is different if you have a little bit of power in your pocket or none at all. What actors have to remember is that we don't work for them. I don't mean that in some power-hungry type of way. You have to find someone who will have your best intentions in mind. I want someone who believes in me before I hit. You have to be with someone who believes in you. But at the same time, you do want them to feel like you're worth their time. So, it's a very vulnerable position to be in. I think it's important to be honest, but not to put out all of your cards in the first fifteen seconds. They're not your shrink. I think the most important thing to do is listen. Don't be uncomfortable in the silence or feel like you have to fill every gap. Let them talk.

How do you prepare for an audition, beginning with getting the sides/script to the actual first audition?

I research it if there's anything to research. If it's a television show, I watch it online. That's what I did with *Grey's [Anatomy.]* I had never seen *Grey's* before, so I watched it online. I watch it to get a sense of the tone. It was Sara who told me to do that. You need to know what type of comedy it is. For example, you should know if there is a laugh track, is it for an audience, what are the inside jokes, do you even know that you're funny. Also, get a sense of the speed, the tone, the tenor, and the timing. All TV & film is not the same. So, I prepare by studying what's available, but really just trying to master the lines, and then figure out what they're saying.

I prepare by looking at the script as if I were the writer to try to figure out why every single word is there. I also want to know what the writer is trying to convey. I don't think I've ever done an audition fully on book, unless the writer is in the room. At the same time, you have to know the rules in order to break the rules. So, I learn the words, and then understand the essence, and then I can be flexible with it. Hours before, I can't really focus on anything else. When I first started auditioning, if I had a 3pm audition, I couldn't have anything before it that day. Your best audition is in the car on the way home from the audition. You'll think to yourself, "Why didn't I do it like that?" So, I think you need to sit with the words for as long as possible.

What is the most important thing a casting director has ever told you?

"That was awful." "You can't just learn the lines." "Why are you looking over there?" All of those were wakeup call moments. We don't walk around with a mirror and an actor has to be a master of his body and language. So, anything where you get some kind of response like that, you have to assess it. The negatives and the criticism are the helpful pieces. The praise doesn't help me at all.

After booking a job, how do you prepare for the role?

It's very similar to auditioning in that I do as much research as possible, but now the writer is going to be there, so really break down the words and figure out why every syllable is there. If it feels redundant, or if you have a real question, go and ask the writer, just to be clear. I'm someone who makes discoveries late. My tenth take was my best take, but I shouldn't need ten, I should need five. So, my goal for the next month would be to try to knock it out in five takes. I just try to be ready and not figure it out on set.

What are the most important things for new actors to know about being on set?

If you have a question, really think about it. But once you think about it and think about it and you still have the same question, go ask it. But don't be desperate. Don't be needy. Don't be constantly fishing for compliments. They already hired you. They want you to succeed more than anybody. Some actors worry, "Why is the director not talking to me?" If the director is not talking to you, he liked it. Actors still have a need for that interaction. But don't ask questions you already know the answer to. Don't ask questions you could've figured out the answer to if you had read your material beforehand. If you want your word to mean something on set, then treat it that way. I think a lot of people just want to interact with that cool director, or executive producer, or writer. So, for example, "Am I really asking this question because we dated before?" "Well, you didn't date before because that was just a dream." "Oh, well, I know" And then the actor is stuck. I know that seems a little abstract, but I see that happen all the time. People are hovering and lingering. Set is an intimidating place. Find some friends. Find a safe place to be. Less is more in interactions on set. You can always linger by craft services later. Do some research on the people you'll be with on set. Maybe you went to the same college as someone. Maybe your sister lives in the same town. They're just people. They have lives. People want to hire people they can stand to be around and people they like to be around.

What's the biggest challenge you face in the entertainment industry?

Realizing that there are different levels of preparedness. If you think you're prepared, but you're tired, you're not prepared. Figuring it out on camera is very risky business Maybe you didn't get it until your fourth take, but guess what, they may need to use that first take because your collar was messed up in the others. So, that take will follow you for the rest of your life. So, take it seriously.

Is there any additional advice you have for other actors? (Especially new actors)

I don't mean this in a scare-tactic way. People often say, "If you can do anything else, do it." I would instead say if you are interested in anything else, *also* do it. Don't quit acting to do it. I need balance in my life and balance in my interests. I can pay attention to two things at once. I can handle politics, sports, and also writing and photography for example. Especially if you live in Los Angeles. There is so much pressure and competition in this town. I don't know if I would've continued to be an actor had I started in LA. Everybody's always having a pissing contest with each other, even best friends. It's a very corrupting experience, so I recommend you seek balance. If you're half ass-ing it or if you're not wholly focused, you're not doing yourself justice. You don't need to be out at a club. You need to be studying to survive. You should be watching the currently working actors to see why they're booking. You don't need to watch Marlon Brando because that's not going to help you book. You need to take it really, really seriously, or you should do something else. But of course, that's coming from the guy who is also telling you to not make it your whole life and to also do other things. Find a balance to make you an interesting person. A lot of the actors I meet who I really admire are interesting people. They look like the kinds of people whom I would want to have a conversation with. Character doesn't come out of good looks. It's a very deep thing. So, you should always be striving for that.

CHRISTINA OCHOA

What advice would you give to new actors, but in particular to women?

Let me start by saying that I hope things are changing for women in this industry. In my personal experience, walking in, apologizing less, asking for less permission, staking claim to my craft and walking in with that energy has served me very well, especially when it comes to audition rooms. Being on set is a whole different ball game. I would say that, particularly for women, once on set it is important to recognize that most people (hopefully) want to be your allies. Rely on those people from a human standpoint, but also be sure that you respect and uphold your own boundaries. What you are comfortable with will be constantly threatened, even if most of the time it could be unintentionally. We need to know where we stand on what, and with whom, because this is a collaborative industry and a lot of it depends on who you are working with. Something I was comfortable with on one project does not mean I am comfortable with this across the board. We as women are often less comfortable holding our ground, and it is something that you absolutely need to be able to do when you are on set.

How would you say the industry has changed over the past two years and where do you see it going from here?

Zero tolerance is a wonderful practice that has developed, especially with movements such as 'Me Too' and 'Time's Up', and that is definitely a positive change I would say that I have noticed. I've also noticed a lot more focus on gender parity in general. The goal is to ultimately not have to have these conversations at all. I've definitely noticed the focus being there, but I'm not sure we always know how to properly address or fix the issues. We have gotten much better at recognizing them. I think there is going to be a trial and error element as far as figuring out what can actually provide us a solution. At the end of the day, I'm very much of the mindset that it requires an underlying structure, not just in this industry, but socially, built around enabling and empowering women from childhood to feel responsible and in ownership of their space, profession, craft, and emotional state, among others.

Do you have a go-to process when it comes to auditioning? Is that different or how does it change when preparing for a role?

I do. I have a lot of little rituals and practices I do for myself. If we can only control two percent of the outcome, we have to make sure that we do everything we can to make sure those two percent represent the best we can offer. As far as rituals go, I don't really run the lines or scenes as much as I work on character and how I can incorporate those specific traits into the scene. I very much massage the text if need be, I try to find beats in the script that allow me to show the characteristics I've highlighted, and if I can't find them, I will make them up and craft them myself. I plan the way I'm going to go to the audition; I try to live like the character, and I try to walk into the room as a very fleshed out character or a fully formed human being. I tend to work out like my character, drive like them, go out and dress like my character, and I've even done therapy sessions as my character, which is a wonderful improv device as well. When it comes to character prep, I love music. I have playlists and soundtracks for them, their essence and who they are. I think they all move differently and rhythm is a really great tool to use. I dance like my characters, and I give them all a horoscope or Myers Briggs, or anything that gives them an easy infusion of personality traits that I don't naturally have. It's all about making it my own and doing things that other people aren't doing in the room. I believe your performance and the choices you've made are enhanced by having a large depth of knowledge about the person you are playing.

If you could give one piece of advice to your 18-year-old self, what would it be?

Hmm. Get into acting sooner? I would probably tell myself that I should try to not be such a know-it-all. I thought I knew exactly where I was going and how I was going to get there, and I wish that I could have had a little bit more fun and not set deadlines for myself. At the same time, I don't really have any regrets about my path, so it is really hard to give myself advice that wouldn't have changed the direction or some of the mistakes

I've made. Because I loved making those mistakes. I've done everything so backwardly and I've really embraced the idea of failure. I wouldn't want to change a lot.

What do you do in your downtime?

What is downtime? I don't know what downtime is. Time where I'm not on set, I spend my time either working on passion projects or advocacy or the philanthropic causes I believe in. I don't have a lot of downtime, and I'm trying to get better at finding what that space looks like for me.

*Note from Sara:

After coaching Christina through her Animal Kingdom audition where her character is having sex, and consequently booking that role which meant filming sex scenes, I worked with her on breaking it down, making it comfortable, and combining the technical with the actual performance. Christina came to me after shooting and said, "I think this should be a class. An important one that all actors, but especially female actors, need to have." This has now become our infamous intimacy class.

How do you deal with intimacy scenes?

Preparation is key. I would say above all, I work those scenes with more attention to detail than I do any others. I work my rapport with my costar, and I choreograph them as specifically as possible, especially the more foreign or unfamiliar I am with that particular actor and set. Once I am comfortable with my costar, I try to build on that trust and knowledge of character, and ensure that all my choices are based on script and character. If I've agreed to take on a role that has intense intimacy or nudity, I did it because I feel that all of those scenes are justified by the character and writing.

Being a woman in Hollywood, what pressures do you feel effect you more than your male counterparts?

There is more pressure to be perfect. We are given less permission to fallible. We pay for our mistakes more heavily. Another difference is that the industry isn't built for our skillsets when it comes to interpersonal communication and the navigation of the political side of the industry. It has been a male dominated arena for a long time, and the way it is built, the foundation it has, is to allow male traits to thrive. The idea of having heart to hearts, or the ability to infuse strength with vulnerability – which is what we see on every breakdown in existence – is not something that is built into the industry as a whole. Now that there are more women behind the camera and moving into positions of power, I think it is going to change.

What do you look for in the script or pitch of a project that you are considering?

Unconventional is something that for me I tend to gravitate towards. Anything that I haven't seen done or seen done well. I like to look at the relationships between characters. Obviously, it all stems from writing, that's the easy answer. If it starts from good writing and that is the jumping off point, that's a great start. But for me, it's more about how the relationships between the characters are crafted, and if the way they are written allows me to give them the amount of subtext I want or whether it's too on the nose. Or also, if the dynamic between them is unique and it's something I haven't seen or explored before. And also, location. Is it filming on a tropical beach?

Is there one type of character you'd really like to play that you haven't had the opportunity to do yet?

There are a number of them! I would love to play a female scientist so that I can avoid some of the tropes and clichés I see on screen. I would love to play a character who is incredibly neurotic, which is something I haven't had the opportunity to do before. I also think it would be fun to play someone from another planet or an alien. So, a neurotic, alien, female scientist is really the dream role now.

Have you ever had a negative on-set experience with an intimacy scene? If so, what actions would you take to not let that happen again?

Because I have previously done nudity or intimacy scenes on shows where it was warranted, I have felt like when I go to other sets, they expected me to be okay with it anything, even if it is over the top or gratuitous. So, I've had to stand my ground and say 'no'. I've felt backed into a corner to comply because I didn't know whether or not I had the right ammunition to argue against something I had already done it. There was definitely an element of feeling peer pressured and manipulated. What I ended up doing was just sticking to my guns. I said that I would do it if it felt right or organic for the character. I'd do it when the writing, crew, directing, and environment on set encouraged me to feel very comfortable and not like a puppet. If the set doesn't encourage that kind of free, creative expression it becomes dirty for me. I went back to the other sets I've been on, and told the people pressuring me that those sets were handled in a way that was respectful to me. I felt comfortable, the director would have conversations with me before shooting, and discuss what my comfort level was. Now it is really easy for me to say 'no' if you just come up to me and say, "Can you just wear this thong for your wardrobe?" Because right now, in this environment, nobody wants to be the one who pushes a woman into doing something they aren't comfortable with.

What helps you get to a place of confidence instead of insecurity when getting ready to film an intimacy scene?

The relationships with my director and costar are really important. People aren't trained on how to build trust in an intimacy scene in both a professional and emotional manner. Knowing my costar has my back, that we are going to check in with each other before or after the scene, that my director has worked with us to choreograph something that we each feel comfortable with, is incredibly important. This all cannot be encouraged enough across the board, but especially for the men on set. You guys can take the lead and make sure the women on set, who already feel more exposed and vulnerable, are comfortable in that environment. Be allies. Make sure that you are not being creepy, do not comment – even if you think it's a compliment – on appearances. Don't crack jokes unless you know you have that rapport with your costar, because they can be taken very differently. It is a sensitive subject and we have to build the relationship of trust first and foremost. Think about how you'd want your sister or your wife to be treated and act accordingly. The same goes for women. We can forget men are also exposed, so after the scene check in with him and make sure he is comfortable as well. I'm very fortunate that the sets on which I have had to do intimacy scenes or nudity have all been incredibly professionally run and that my costars have been equally enthusiastic at looking at the choreography from a place that is both character building and driven.

Do potential intimacy scenes and or nudity inform which projects you are interested in? If so, what are the factors that go into that?

The only thing I would say is that if the intimacy or nudity is gratuitous, for me, that's an indicator of how the rest of the script or the set is going to be. The nudity is a kind of litmus test for whether or not the character is crafted in a complex, nuanced manner. There may be scripts I read where she's immediately walking out of the shower naked, and that doesn't really make sense for an ABC network comedy, so that probably says the writing or project isn't going to be great.

Is there anything else you'd like to add or say?

I would say the one thing we haven't touched on that, to me, is really important is finding a support system within the industry. Finding colleagues and mentors is invaluable. Sara is great at doing that for 'her girls', and that is very important. There's something I've noticed a lot where, once someone is working or has moderate success, the men are all hanging out, or friends, or going out for beer, regardless of whether they are competing with each other or not. The women, for the most part, are not. I think it is still ingrained in us, in a weird way as women – not to necessarily compete with each other – but that we still need to do it on our own. There is a kind of survivor mentality. We need to find mentors, find people you want to help, and make sure that you don't become myopic by embracing that role and helping others, allowing others to help you, and embracing that sense of community.

SHERRY THOMAS

What advice do you have for actors who just moved to Los Angeles?

There is a lot to this question. It depends on the situation. If someone is coming from a background of training, for example, if they've just completed a program in school or any kind of extended period of training, they should continue that training. I think the biggest mistake actors make is rushing to LA and thinking, "oh my god, I need headshots because I'm going to start auditioning." I think so many people who take that approach are not necessarily ready to be in a room with a casting director auditioning or meeting agents or managers. A common mistake is to not learn the business side of the industry. Learning the craft of acting doesn't necessarily mean you're ready for the business side of acting.

What can actors expect at their first audition?

The first time is probably going to be very nerve-wracking. Possibly unpleasant, possibly amazing. It just depends on the office that you're going to. You need to do your homework about the project you're going in on and the background of the casting director. Know if you will be seeing the casting director, the casting associate, or the casting assistant. It's not that it matters because the process should be the same; it's just good to have as much information as possible.

Be as prepared as possible. Just be yourself. I think so often, people read what a role is and they have perceptions of what they think they should be and what hooker #1 is to one show is not what hooker #1 is to another show or another person. And I'm not sure why I used that example, but I did. It's just an extension of who you are. Remember that casting offices are very busy. If you call to ask details, they may get snippy and snap at whoever's on the other end. I don't think that would happen at my office, but it's important to be prepared for that.

What are some of the smarter choices you've seen actors make in the room? How far is too far to go with a choice in the room?

Don't bring a fake gun. The choices depend on a number of factors, including the role and the project. I want to see a believable interpretation of the role, and if for that person, that means that they have to hold up their hand and pretend they're holding a gun, great. But it better look believable. It has to be in the moment and it has to be a part of that scene and real. The whole thing about acting is to make it real. I've almost been punched a couple of times and it didn't bother me so much, but it bothered my producers who were in the room and it made them feel very uncomfortable. I think that you have to respect the other person's space. If you feel that you have to take it to that place, then you need to ask the casting director before you do it. Are you comfortable if, in the moment, I feel like I want to x, y, and z? To me, what goes into making a smart choice is feeling confident enough to know that you might want to go to that place and is that okay? They may say no, and then you have to deal with it.

What are some common mistakes you see actors making on their resumes?

Lying, lying, and lying. If you're honest and truthful, the work will speak for itself. Work begets work, begets work. Just because you have a full resume doesn't mean you're a good actor. If I may be so bold. I also think that sometimes, when an actor is relatively new to the business side of it, they feel like they have to stack it so it looks full and they enhance it in a way that it just looks junior high – high school. And putting too much personal information because, sadly, there are a lot of crazies out there who are not entirely ethical. You don't want your very personal phone number or email address or address. On the flip side of that, we've gotten many resumes from people we really wanted to meet and there is no contact information on it. Get somebody to double-check your work.

What (if anything) should actors do differently from an initial audition to the callback? Should they wear the same thing?

If in the initial pre-read, you wear jeans and a t-shirt, should you then, in your callback, wear a Prada suit? No, I think probably not. You can change your top, but don't change the look because that might've been what worked. For me, I'm always so direct and straightforward that if I want you to wear something different, I'm going to tell you. So if I don't, similar or the same to what you're wearing is great. Again, I think it's more about the work than the look, but to a degree obviously. For example, if the role is for an attractive person, then you need to come in looking attractive. If it's for a busty, va-va-voom role, don't come in wearing a sports bra that will push your boobs down. I feel like so much of this is common sense.

What has changed about the industry from your perspective in the last ten years?

So much is being cast from tape and not from actors actually being in the room. You don't want to shoot up; you always want to shoot level. You want to make sure that the reader is a little off to one side or the other, so you're cheating a little and not looking directly into the camera, unless the role breaks the third wall, in which case, you can look directly into camera. Specifically for self-taping, you want to make sure it's a solid background and that you do a full body shot with your slate separate [from] the read. Shoot from about the chest up. Make sure the volume is good. We do not ever allow anyone to be transferred through YouTube because most places don't want their material out for the entire world to see, again common sense. If you're going in to be on tape, we most often say it's just going on tape for the producers, and then, just make sure your makeup is a little more camera ready, but not totally done. Remember that you won't have a huge space to be mobile in.

Another change is that established actors have more of an ego about pre- reading when in fact, as a casting director, I think we're trying to protect the actor and make sure they're right for the role by not wasting the producer's time and not showing them in a light that's not right for them. If they can't handle the size of the role, it's our job to figure that out beforehand. If they're not right for the role, what they should be thinking is, "If the CD wants to work with me, and if I'm not completely right for the role, they're not going to bring me back and make me look like an ass in front of the producers, that's awesome.

Do you have any advice for actors about their reels?

I prefer to see quality, not quantity. Again, it's kind of like with a resume, quite often, actors don't have tape on themselves yet, so they run out and produce a demo reel with their friends and the scene is one I know very well from a movie. You have to be a very good actor to do that. Otherwise, it just looks like a high school project. And it's hard because I know actors are doing everything they can to be proactive. I understand it. Showing me three, one-line roles that you've done on actual television shows, as opposed to one long scene that you created in a park, I'd rather see the three one-line roles. It's all working from a place of fear, rather than a place where you are today. Are you really ready to be a series regular just having moved to Los Angeles? Probably not. But there are those cases. In the fifteen years that I've been doing this, I know of two people who flew out here for pilot season and booked a series regular. And both had gone to school and trained beforehand.

When an actor is labeled green, what does that mean to you?

Not experienced. They make a lot of the mistakes. There might be something interesting there and they just need experience in class or experience auditioning or experience just with material.

Is there anything you think might surprise people about being a casting director?

How hard it is. How labor intensive it is. Don't get me wrong, it is not brain surgery, but it's not just, la-la-la, so fun, actors reading in a room. Everything is a piece of a puzzle and you want that puzzle to be magnificent when you're done. Or if it's a painting, you want to make sure all the colors are working together.

How much and in what forms do you electronically research actors you are considering?

If I'm passionate about an actor and they don't have a reel, I will go to YouTube and see if there are any clips from anything else they have done. I will Google. I will do whatever I need to do. If I see a movie and I don't know an actor, then I first go to IMDb, but then I do as much research as possible. I don't really use Facebook as a form of actor research and I never really used MySpace either. Mostly, just Google, IMDb, and YouTube. It is the wave of the future; it's how it's being done now. I think if an aspiring actor has a website, that's fantastic.

What makes a great headshot?

A real representation of the person is what I want to see. I don't care if it's color or black and white. I think way too much thought goes into that. I just want it to be a good shot and representative of what I want to see.

What would you think if an actor followed up with you after, perhaps in the form of a thank you note? And how do you feel about postcards?

I think postcards are fantastic. I think stalking postcards are annoying, so don't stalk. But if there's something legitimately going on in your world and you want to share that, I think it's great. I think thank you cards are lovely too. I don't have any problem with that whatsoever. But, if there's nothing to thank me for, don't send one. I just don't like the bullshit. I want sincerity in the work, in everything. I have not cast people because I didn't like them as people. When you're working together on a series, those people become your family. I have had several shows I've worked on where people come to me and say, "How did you do it? There's just not an asshole in the bunch." I'm not saying everybody's perfect; everybody has his or her moments. But generally, we've gotten amazing reports back from the sets, saying how wonderful the experience was.

What is the best demeanor to have when entering the room? More confident and focused or nice and easy to work with?

I think you have to come in with whatever mindset works for you. We have invited you in to do a job for us, so while some CD's might flip it and have a bit of an ego, as if to say, "perform for me; impress me," the only reason you're there in our office is because we asked you to come.

What are your thoughts about being off book?

I think it depends on your ability. Even if you're off book, you have the sides with you. It just reminds everyone that you're not on set. We have a saying in our office that it doesn't have to be perfect until you're getting paid. And anything up to that point is a work in progress. If it's one line, it's probably best to be off book. The two biggest mistakes an actor can make are one, making excuses from the moment you walk in the door. If I have a question about the reading that just took place in terms of the prep, I'll ask, and then you can tell me. You can make up an excuse or tell the truth, whatever you want to do. But to walk in and start with the excuses, you're just projecting that you're going to do poorly. "I just got this, I worked until three a.m., etc." If you're going to walk in and try to do that, then perhaps, you should've tried to reschedule. Two, when you're finished and the CD is saying thank you, to then say, "is there anything you want to see different?" If there were anything we wanted to see you do differently, we would've probably asked you to do it differently. That's different than saying, "fuck; that sucked. Can I do it differently?" And they may say no, and if they do, you leave. Otherwise, you're not listening to me when I say I've gotten everything I want from you. It becomes about your ego and I'm not there to pat you on the head. We're both there to do a job.

Would you like it if someone came and said, I've prepared it two different ways. Would you like to see it A or B?

I always say, make a choice. I might say, "let's try B." Then, I might say, "let's try A." Or I might say, "Why don't you decide?" And then I might still give them the other adjustment. Or, sometimes when you're doing a pilot and you're reading so many people, I might just give a note prior and say, "here's the trap of the scene... do me a favor, why don't you play it like this..." Because they've only prepared it one way, they might not have the ability to take that note. And that's okay. Then they're just not ready.

How did you become a casting director?

I came out here from Massachusetts in my *Toyota Tercel*. I fell into it, literally. I was a manager at the *Gap* and I started doing some work for a charity that Mary Jo Slater was doing at the time and Victoria Burrows worked in the same suite as her. And I became friendly with Victoria Burrows and she said, "When you're done with Mary Jo, if you want to intern as a casting intern, just let me know." And I said, "yeah!" Because I listened to what was going on in the casting office and I understood it. I got it. I knew I wanted to work in the industry; I just wasn't sure where.

Because I came from a performance background, I thought I'd naturally transfer into acting, but it just wasn't the proper fit for me at the time. I started interning in casting and I loved it. And then, my first job was with a location CD on the movie *Contact*. Then, it just went from there and I worked my way up. I just loved everything about it. And I could take my strength as a performer and put it into the work of a casting director. I also came from a management background, so I knew how to manage people and be business-like. I think there are so many people in this industry who don't have any idea about that. They don't know how to manage people effectively. Because I worked in retail management for two of the biggest companies, they spent millions and millions of dollars teaching their managers how to better manage. And it's just so necessary. The people who are yellers and screamers, it's because they don't have any other skills on how to communicate what should and shouldn't be done.

If there isn't a camera in the room, what, if anything, should actors do differently?

Nothing. But there are certain things to remember for tape. Knowing how much room you have on tape is maybe good. Remember that you're not just auditioning for this role; you're auditioning for this CD.

Would you like for an actor to compliment your work when he enters the room?

If they're saying something just to blow smoke up my ass, don't say it. If you are a huge fan of *Breaking Bad*, for example, and you would like to say something, that's fine. But don't say that just because it's what you think I want to hear.

ABOUT THE AUTHOR

Sara Mornell is the President and CEO of Mornell Studios, LLC, a female-driven entertainment hub in Atlanta that aims to uplift the world through empowered artists and activism. She is also a renowned acting coach, author, director, public speaker, and has been a Hollywood actor for the past 25 years.

At the height of her acting career, while recurring on two network shows, and appearing on a pilot, Mornell made a powerful pivot toward coaching. Working with actors like Jesse Williams, Christina Ochoa, Tessa Thompson, and thousands more, Mornell quickly became the antidote to the antiquated methodology of theater techniques which do not translate to working in Hollywood today. The existing training modalities, while big business, do not serve actors seeking work in today's Film & TV landscape. So, the Mornell Method, a groundbreaking radically new method, was born to fill that void.

Mornell has been successfully coaching actors, athletes and entertainers for the past 11 years with her Mornell Method, which utilizes the rigor and focused mindset of athletic training, while empowering artists to find their authentic voice. As a coach, Mornell is known for changing actors' lives by guiding them to step into their power and launch into super stardom.

In 2016, Mornell left Los Angeles to open a production studio in Atlanta, GA that would also house her two year acting program. The program trains actors for TV and film and takes a novice to a working actor in under three years. She's taken cues from former co-stars and similarly aligned activists like Ted Dansen, whom she co-starred with on Becker , and George Clooney, with whom she shot a pilot for HBO; and inspiration from women like Oprah Winfrey and Reese Witherspoon who use the power of their platforms to make a bigger impact in the world and to pave the way for more female directors, cinematographers, writers, and producers.

Mornell also works with Apple to help their artists develop their voice, and has started two non-profits. In 2019, Mornell created a non-profit foundation that gives talented individuals from all backgrounds and genders, specifically BIPOC, an equal chance to succeed with access to quality training. She also started WWOMM, a free support community for women who suffer and want to free themselves from a traumatic relationship with their mother.

Mornell's drive to give back, empower, serve, and uplift is the fuel that keeps this media mogul running. When she's not working (which is rare!), Mornell enjoys hanging out with her partner and their three dogs, working out, doing yoga, and reading.

@MornellStudios

@SaraMornell

@ MornellStudiosProductions

@mornellStudios

@SaraMornell

www.mornellstudios.com

Made in the USA
Columbia, SC
15 November 2023